BUNYIPS IN THE CLASSROOM: THE 10 CHANGES

The moral right of the author has been asserted. This book is copyright. Apart from any fair dealing for the purpose of private study, research, criticism or review, as permitted under the *Copyright Act*, no part of this book may be reproduced by any process without written permission.

Published by
Literacy Plus Australia
Mackay QLD 4740
AUSTRALIA

© Susan Galletly 2022
First published 2022

www.susangalletly.com

 A catalogue record for this work is available from the National Library of Australia

Title: Bunyips in the Classroom

Subtitle: The 10 Changes

Author: Galletly, Susan

ISBNs: 9780957705968 (paperback)

            9780957705975 (ebook – epub)

            9780645535303 (ebook – Kindle)

Subjects: **EDUCATION** / Educational Policy & Reform / General;
            POLITICAL SCIENCE / World / Australian & Oceanian;
            LANGUAGE ARTS & DISCIPLINES / Reading Skills;
            FAMILY & RELATIONSHIPS / Learning Disabilities

All reasonable efforts were taken to obtain permission to use copyright material reproduced in this book, but in some cases copyright could not be traced. The author welcomes information in this regard.

Cover design by Yes Peach Creative at yespeach.com.au

Cover art by Alana Smith, Temperance Art

The Yuwi people are the traditional custodians of the land where this book was written. The author pays her respects to elders and people past, present, and future, across Australia; and honours the traditions of the Aboriginal, Torres Strait Islander, Solomon Islander and Vanuatuan people. She acknowledges, respects and greatly regrets the major wrongs our first nations peoples have experienced, due to, and as part of, white settlement.

BUNYIPS IN THE CLASSROOM: THE 10 CHANGES

Dr Susan Galletly

BSpThy, MEd, PhD

Contents

PART 1 SETTING THE SCENE
    An Informal Aussie Glossary 3
    Welcome 7
    The 10 Changes, ABCs and Mantra 12
    Who Am I? 15
    Snapshots of Our Struggles 19
    Our Sad Bad Early Years Factory 27
    The Massive Differences Orthographies Make 33
    Orthographic Complexity Can Be Managed Well 46
    Our Struggling-Education Problem 53
    Our Disappointing Reading Results 64
    Let's Solve This! 76

PART 2 THE 10 CHANGES
    Setting Our Goals 81
    Change 1 Understand How Orthographies Matter 84
    Change 2 Own Our Struggling Reader Woes 98
    Change 3 Weigh Workload 113
    Change 4 Respect Learning Differences 136
    Change 5 Investigate Word-Reading 149
    Change 6 Enrich Education for Every Child 165
    Change 7 Insist on Easier Literacy Development 173
    Change 8 Investigate Beginners' Orthographies 183
    Change 9 Play to Enrich Language and Learning 196
    Change 10 Build Useful Research Knowledge 210

PART 3 INTO THE FUTURE WE GO
    Let's Work Upstream and Down 223
    Keep Change Thinking Happening 227

For our struggling Aussie readers –
Our Spelling Generations.
Never think you're failures:
You're victims of English orthographic complexity,
And the inadequate education we've provided.
Our education support strategies are the failures:
The ones that have failed so badly to meet your needs.

For our struggling Aussie teachers,
Working far too hard, amidst inadequate resourcing.
Thank you so much! You're world class!

And for Australia, our beloved nation.
How wonderful to live here with Aussies all,
In our beautiful land, and precious democracy,
Where one can speak openly and honestly.

With many thanks to our wonderful God,
Who guides and leads.

There are no such things as reading difficulties.

There are only teaching challenges.

Jackie French[i], Children's Laureate 2014-15
Acceptance Speech for the award of
2015 Senior Australian of the Year

PART 1
SETTING THE SCENE

An Informal Aussie Glossary

Bunyips, Elephants, Koalas and Kids

Elephant in the Room
A big embarrassing issue people are very aware of, which is deliberately not mentioned.

Bunyip
An Aussie creature some consider mythical and monstrous.

Bunyip in the Room
A big issue that people aren't aware of, which is extremely obvious once it's explained, and well worth considerable embarrassment for having been largely ignored.

Cute Koalas
Koalas are precious Australian creatures well worth our love, protection and best supports. So too are Aussie kids. Young koalas are called joeys. In this book's colloquial vein, I at times refer to our precious children as *cute koalas*. *Joeys* are our young children in their first school years. *Crushed and crumpled koalas* are our struggling readers, crumpled by the inadequate education they've received.

Kids
It's not just goats that have kids. Aussie parents have them too. We often refer to our children and students as kids.

Orthographies: Spelling Systems

Orthographies

The spelling systems that nations choose to use. Standard Australian English is our official Australian orthography.

English Orthographic Complexity

Standard English orthography is one of the world's most complex spelling systems. English orthographic complexity makes learning to read and write complicated, vastly more difficult than most nations, and extremely slow to develop.

Orthographic Advantage

Advantages regular-orthography nations enjoy, which build from their easy, rapid, early-literacy development.

Regular-orthography nations are the world's many nations that have chosen to use highly regular spelling systems, e.g., Finland, Estonia, Netherlands, Italy, Spain, Greece, Poland, Wales, South Korea, Taiwan, Japan and China.

Orthographic Disadvantage

The education and life struggles we have, due to English orthographic complexity, our slow, drawn-out early-literacy development, and our having too many struggling readers.

Of Thirds, Years and Grades

Thirds

A useful way to collectively consider our kids and their learning needs. Our upper-third are stronger readers and learners, our middle-third kids are average achievers, and our lower-third are our weaker readers and learners.

Years vs Grades

We say *Year 1*, while many other nations say *Grade 1*. In this book, the word *Year* is used to refer to Australian school years, while *Grade* is used for other nations.

Cognitive Load and Cognitive Processing

Cognitive Load
The amount we have to think on at any one time. English orthographic complexity creates high cognitive load for our kids, across the years they're learning to read and write.

Cognitive-Processing Skills
Cognitive-processing skills include short-term, working and long-term memory, executive-function skills, orthographic awareness, and phonological and phonemic awareness. Our kids need them for mastering complex Standard English.

Working Memory
The functional processing capacity we use when thinking. It's much needed for our joeys learning to read and write.

Our Education Woes

Spelling Generations
Our generations of Aussie kids and adults with sadly low reading, writing and literacy skills.

Struggling Readers
A catch-all term for our children and adults with literacy difficulties: while many start with word-reading difficulties, this usually evolves to soon include struggles with reading, spelling, writing and subject-area learning.

Swiss-Cheese Research Areas
Important research topics (a strong cheese flavour) where we've more knowledge gaps than solid research findings (more holes than cheese) – and strong needs for research.

Our Early Years Factory
Our first three school years, Foundation (which many states call Prep) through Year 2, which produce both our struggling readers and our education struggles.

Our Find the Learning Time Challenge

Because we spend such long hours building word-reading and spelling, our schools are time-poor, and our teachers struggle to find sufficient time to teach thoroughly.

Our Find the Caring Time Challenge

Our schools being time-poor means our kids often miss out on mentoring and the social-emotional supports they need.

Our Language-Weakness Epidemic

In Australia, weak language skills are widespread. Kids with weak language skills often become struggling readers.

WYSYAIN (*wise-yain*)

My acronym for *What You See, You Assume Is Normal*. In ignoring regular-orthography nations, we've done lots of WYSYAINing. It makes for many bunyips in the classroom.

Our Needs for Major Improvement

Es and Cs of Advantage vs Disadvantage

Regular-orthography nations enjoy Es: Easy, Expedited, Efficient, Effective Education that's relatively Effortless too. We've sad Cs: Confused, Complicated, Chaotic learning.

GENTLE

My acronym for *Gentle, Engaging, Never-Tiring, Learning Enrichment*. Finland and Estonia evidence it well.

HEARTSH

My acronym for the *Hugely-Exhausting, Actually-Rather-Tedious Schooling Heaviness*. It's common in Australian schools, particularly for our struggling readers.

The 10 Changes

Ten strategic changes Australia needs, to exponentially improve literacy development and education, by closing our Early Years Factory and ending our Spelling Generations.

Welcome

All who have meditated on the art of governing mankind have been convinced that the fate of empires depends on the education of youth.

Aristotle[ii]

Hello and welcome.

Across the decades, I've been closely observing education, and our struggles, and how our difficulties contrast so markedly with the successes so many other nations enjoy.

I'd like to discuss with you 10 Changes – key directions Australian education needs to explore, to exponentially improve the education we provide for our cute koala kids.

Bunyips in the Classroom: The 10 Changes is small, but it packs a punch in the points it raises. You'll find most points very logical, while a few may initially seem somewhat out of left field.

In Australian education, we've lots of bunyips in our classrooms. While an elephant in the room is incredibly obvious, a bunyip in the room hasn't been noticed. Once pointed out, however, it's blatantly obvious and clearly an important issue – and one well worth squirming about, as it feels both absurd and embarrassing that it could have been overlooked for so long.

I'll point out quite a few bunyips across this book. I'll also point out what I term WYSYAIN (*wise-yain*), my acronym for *What You See, You Assume Is Normal*. In education here, we've done considerable WYSYAINing.

We WYSYAIN when we consider our education situation the norm and assume things are similar in nations everywhere. In reality, by international standards, we have far too many struggling readers, plus our children's reading and writing development is appallingly slow.

A *Time Magazine* article by Unmesh Kher in 2001 discussing reading difficulties in Italy and USA, opened my eyes to the importance of orthographies (spelling systems), and how things are very different in regular-orthography nations.

As Kher[iii] stated,
> *English has 1120 different ways of spelling its 40 phonemes, the sounds required to pronounce all its words. By contrast, Italian needs only 33 combinations of letters to spell out its 25 phonemes. ...*
> *The reported rate of dyslexia in Italy is barely half that in the US where 15% are affected to varying degrees.*

As I investigated further, I learned more and more about the very major differences between us and regular-orthography nations. Nations can choose the orthographies they use and, unlike us and other Anglophone nations, most nations have sensibly chosen highly-regular orthographies.

Further, Korea, Taiwan, Japan and China, nations with orthographies far more complex than ours, which previously had far more major literacy struggles than ours, introduced their beginners' orthographies in the 20th Century. This quickly resolved their literacy difficulties and precipitated massive educational and economic growth.

Importantly, our kids wrestle with Standard English and its complexities, with slow arduous learning and many kids struggling; but virtually all regular-orthography kids thrive and are soon confidently literate – even their kids who start school with what would be major risk factors here.

Suffice to say Kher's article confronted my WYSYAINing on that area with sledgehammer force, and it steadily ground to a halt, as I learned more and more.

Welcome

As we explore bunyips and the 10 Changes across this book, you'll build awareness of the WYSYAINing we do, and our major needs for change.

Some of my recommendations may seem overly ambitious. They're not. They're totally achievable and realistic. We have wonderful potential to do far better, brilliantly in fact.

My passionate hope is that the many issues we touch on will excite your interest. Then, you too will be actively thinking on the three key wonderings that have guided my enquiries and learning:

- What factors cause our kids and adults' reading and literacy difficulties?
- How can we reduce their struggles and suffering?
- What are the ways we can do things better?

They're good questions that are well worth reflecting on and discussing with friends and colleagues.

It will bring me joy to have our bunyips and 10 Changes issues considered and explored, as to date they've had insufficient airplay. Indeed, while they have an extensive research base, some may seem quite new to you.

They're issues to reflect on, and for Australian education to then investigate, then take research through to practice in Aussie schools and classrooms.

Those three questions have guided my thinking and research down the years.

Currently, answers exist, but too many of them are in mere fledgling form.

As an example, it's well established that it's far easier to prevent word-reading difficulties than to remediate difficulties once they're entrenched. But, despite this, we continue to have excessive numbers of struggling readers of all ages with entrenched difficulties we failed to prevent.

Clearer understanding will be established increasingly into the future, through our considering and investigating 10 Changes issues. They need thorough research.

We've too many areas of *Swiss-cheese research*: my term for important research topics (a strong cheese flavour) that have sadly large knowledge gaps (more holes than cheese).

Many issues I discuss aren't specifically Aussie: they're endemic to all English-speaking nations, i.e., Anglophone nations. My focus is overwhelmingly on Australia, however.

We've key problems that are specifically ours, plus education here differs in many ways from that of other nations, e.g., in school resourcing, in teaching practices and in how we develop curriculum at school level.

The issues I'm presenting are logical. They build from both my extensive research knowledge and my many decades of practical experience working with cute koalas with literacy difficulties. Theory plus practice are a particularly powerful combination – they strengthen the confidence and the conviction with which I write.

It's not just my theorising I'm discussing here, of course. It also includes the theorising of our Central Queensland University (CQU) research team, headed by Professor Bruce Knight, with whom I've so enjoyed working. Many thanks to Bruce and other colleagues, notably Professor John Dekkers and Dr Pamela Gargett. Our research publications are available through university libraries and online. You can also download final draft versions from ResearchGate, a research website where many researchers post articles and files for free download.

I've also built from ideas I've gained from the many teachers, children and families I've worked with.

Heartfelt thanks to each and every one of you. So often, when I say *I*, I mean *we*.

While I'll be found spot-on for most suggestions, I may not be completely so for all. That's the nature of research knowledge-building, particularly when we've lots of research that's needed, but hasn't yet been done.

Never do I say this is what we MUST do. Nor do I say the issues and solutions I propose are the sole issues and sole answers for all our education struggles. After all, there's far more to education here than the issues I'm discussing.

But I do say these issues are of sufficient importance that they MUST be considered and investigated. To continue to overlook them would be to do Australian education and our cute koala kids an immense and harsh disservice.

This book is the first in the *Aussie Reading Woes* trilogy:
- Bunyips in the Classroom: The 10 Changes.
- The Research Tours: The Impacts of Orthographic Disadvantage.
- The 10 Changes: The Nitty Gritty.

Each is a separate read, not dependent on its partners. You might read one, two or all of them, in no set reading order.

This book, *Bunyips in the Classroom*, introduces the area.

The Research Tours explores key studies that provide a strong rationale for the 10 Changes, and suggests needed key directions. It details considerable research evidence underlying the discussion of this book and *The Nitty Gritty*.

The 10 Changes: The Nitty Gritty expands on the topics in this book and *The Research Tours*, providing useful detail on orthographic complexity, the 10 Changes, and many other associated issues that readers might wonder on after reading *Bunyips in the Classroom* or *The Research Tours*.

The 10 Changes, ABCs and Mantra

The 10 Changes are key changes that Australian education needs to pursue, to achieve improved reading, early-literacy development and education.

I'll list them here, along with useful ABCs for improving education, and a wise mantra we can use to guide us on our improvement journey.

The 10 Changes

Here are the 10 Changes – our paths to strategic progress:

Change 1. Understand how orthographies matter: English spelling is dragging us down.

Change 2. Own our struggling reader woes: End hypocrisy and pretence.

Change 3. Weigh workload: Our children and teachers are working far too hard.

Change 4. One-size education does not fit all: Teach to the decidedly different instructional needs of upper-third and lower-third readers.

Change 5. End our data deficiency: Build strong knowledge on word-reading levels.

Change 6. Enrich every child: Ensure effective, supportive, tailored education.

Change 7. Insist on easier early-literacy development: Reach regular-orthography nations' achievement levels.

Change 8. Investigate the potential of fully-regular beginners' orthographies: Research shows they're key.

Change 9. First, play to learn: Start Standard English word-reading instruction from mid-Year 2.

Change 10. Build needed research knowledge as quickly as possible: Use collaborative school-based research.

While some of these changes might seem a surprise now, they'll likely be our norm in future decades.

It's interesting how quickly and radically things can change when needed. That's been highlighted by Covid-19 changes. We've developed useful changeability skills, and can now change impressively quickly when we see the need.

So many things seem utterly impossible, until they've been actioned. As Nelson Mandela[iv] stated so wisely: *It always seems impossible until it's done.* Of course, the changes always were possible; they just seemed impossible. That happens easily when WYSYAINing is in full flood.

Our ABCs

Here are the ABCs of our improving of education:

A. ACT locally while looking globally.

B. BOOST the lower-third to benefit everyone.

C. CHANGE effectively to work less and achieve more.

The Mantra for Our Effective Change Journey

Jackie French, our 2014-15 Children's Laureate, historian and prolific author of wonderful books for children and adults, is dyslexic. She understands first-hand the trauma and difficulties that our struggling readers experience.

She sees these difficulties as optional and avoidable.

So do I.

I love the statement she made in her acceptance speech for the 2015 Older Australian of the Year award[v]:

> *There are no such things as reading difficulties.*
> *There are only teaching challenges.*

That's true, very true.

Let's use Jackie's wise words as our mantra for Australia's journey to achieve effective change.

For the vast majority of children, reading difficulties are optional, an education outcome we produce when we don't meet our teaching challenges effectively, through our preventing of difficulties, or quickly overcoming them.

Unlike us, many nations meet their teaching challenges extremely well, for word-reading, spelling, early-literacy and subject-area learning. Across those nations, children quickly become confident, literate, effective learners, and schools consistently and routinely prevent major word-reading and spelling difficulties, and quickly and efficiently overcome the minor difficulties some children experience.

At the current time, we all too often fail to meet our teaching challenges. We've thus far more struggling readers and vastly more severe literacy difficulties than nations that use regular orthographies.

Using 10 Changes improvements, we can change that, impressively.

Who Am I?

Some men see things as they are and say, "Why?"
I dream of things that never were and say, "Why not?"

George Bernard Shaw paraphrased by Robert F Kennedy[vi]

Why am I so confident about what we should do?

Let me explain.

I'm Dr Susan Galletly, an Australian literacy-development and learning-difficulties specialist and researcher, who is also a speech language pathologist and teacher.

In the discussion of this book, I'm building strongly from both research and practice.

In my research work, I've explored education here and internationally, observing education in schools and speaking with teachers and researchers in many nations, including England, Estonia, Finland, Italy, Israel, Japan, South Korea, Taiwan, Thailand, Uganda, USA and Wales.

In my private-practice work across the past four decades, I've worked with many hundreds of struggling learners and their families.

I've also worked extensively with teachers – in research projects, in professional development I've presented, and in working together supporting struggling readers.

Across my career, I've pondered and theorised, exploring theory and practice in education here and elsewhere.

I'm persistent in taking theory through into practice.

I've loved my work. It's been somewhat Edison's[vii] *I never did a day's work in my life. It was all fun.*

I'm a proud and patriotic Australian. I'm confident we've enormous potential for brilliant education into the future.

I've also deep understanding of learning difficulties as I've somewhat similar difficulties myself, from a mild head-injury I acquired when in my thirties. I understand well the intricacies of weak working memory, the stresses that high cognitive load and overload create, and how these can impact learning in nasty ways for at-risk and struggling readers.

I'm a huge admirer of Australian teachers: the hard work they do and the results they achieve, particularly given we overwork them badly in our inadequately resourced schools. Our teachers are among the world's hardest working and best professionals.

My initial training was as a speech language pathologist. I graduated in 1975. I completed extra psychology studies, prior to and after graduation, and was going to also become a psychologist, but then sidestepped into education – the best move I ever made.

I'd always been fascinated by how teachers teach kids to read. Enter stage left, one non-reader, the teacher does wonderful teaching, and, voilà, the child is now a reader, and ofttimes a voracious reader.

And I learned how to do it, to teach kids to read and love reading! Clearly, teaching kids to read was a passion for me, one I'd not yet recognised.

Originally, I'd planned to teach in primary schools for several years, to experience education and school life for successful learners. Already knowing quite a bit about struggling readers, I wanted the broader picture.

Alas, with a glut of teachers at that time, and my having speech language pathology and psychology skills, I not surprisingly found myself employed in Special Education.

I regret I missed out on primary-school teaching then. Over the years, I've done a small amount of primary and high-school teaching. I've also worked as a literacy advisor in primary and high schools, and conducted considerable professional development for teachers across Australia.

Importantly, I've also worked with teachers and schools in collaborative research projects. University researchers and teachers working together, learning from and with each other, so often results in powerful knowledge-building. I love collaborative research.

I've also conducted research on word-reading development, difficulties and instruction, in my Masters and Doctoral studies, then in postdoctoral research work.

Additionally, I spent some years as a university lecturer, lecturing and writing literacy courses for preservice teachers. It's always a privilege to be involved in supporting teachers, and I loved my years of lecturing.

At least half my career has been as a speech language pathologist in private practice, working with kids with literacy learning difficulties and their families. As part of that, I've written books of games and activities for parents and teachers to help kids with word-reading: *Sounds & Vowels*, *Two Vowels Talking* and *Phonological Fun*. Speech language pathology, a fair dose of psychology, and teacher training have proved a powerful combination.

When working with struggling readers, I work one-on-one and use a parent-tutor model, with parents sitting in on all sessions, and families aiming for 90 minutes home practice weekly. We're a team that moves, over time, to me being needed less and less, as kids progress, and parents are increasingly empowered to support their learning journey. Sometimes, kids' teachers or teacher aides attend sessions too, resulting in useful discussions that empower us all.

The children and families who I've worked with are a key motivation for my writing now. I know the suffering that our struggling readers go through daily – it's dreadful and unrelenting! And in their struggles, I see the insufficiencies of the education they're receiving, and how, for so many cute koala kids, we're not meeting our teaching challenges.

Their struggles also highlight how poorly resourced our schools are, and how badly we overwork our teachers.

Australian education has many wonderful strengths, but also key weaknesses where we need massive improvement.

The kids' struggles show how enormously difficult it is for our teachers to successfully catch-up our struggling readers to healthy progress. That's a bunyip.

I know this because in so many instances I've worked with the kids' teachers in other projects, and they're excellent teachers who are highly skilled.

Our kids' learning struggles also highlight the damaging insufficiencies of our inadequate government-funded allied-health services. Another bunyip. Most kids who come to work with me have been in urgent need of free speech language pathology, occupational therapy and psychology intervention, prior to and across the school years – but they've not received these services.

If we're to achieve exponentially-improved education and child development in Australia, it's vital we ease reading and literacy development for all our cute koala kids, particularly our lower-third – our at-risk and struggling readers.

We must also improve our levels of allied-health services. Studies explored in *The Research Tours* show that we've an epidemic of kids with weak language skills, with far too many kids not receiving needed supports. Another bunyip.

Public perception is that free government speech language pathology and occupational therapy services are readily available, along with ample learning-support services. The reality is sadly different: our vulnerable cute koalas miss out on needed supports, left, right and centre.

The 10 Changes are important and very much needed, as massive improvement in many dimensions of education is very much needed here.

Snapshots of Our Struggles

School was a struggle; it was really hard work ... a lot of extra work, a lot of extra classes, a lot of frustration and sometimes screaming at whoever it was that was making me feel like I wasn't good enough.

Orlando Bloom[viii]

What are we up against?

Wasteful, unnecessary, destructive reading and writing difficulties with their debilitating impacts on far too many Australians:
- School years of low achievement, discouragement and low-self-esteem.
- Adult years of diminished career prospects, embarrassment, and feeling *dumb*.
- Reading difficulties leading to reading difficulties: parents nervous of school, and unable to confidently read with their kids and support their school learning.
- Education woes due to our kids and teachers' excessive workload, and time-pressure created by too slow early-literacy development and too many struggling readers.

These challenges are worthy of our best efforts!

Let's consider a few Aussies with whom I've worked, whose experiences very much reflect the everyday struggles that are happening everywhere, across Australian schools.

They might highlight a few bunyips for some of us.

Mattie, Age 9

Mattie's wetting the bed again, his mum informed me. That was finished, but he's just so anxious starting at his new school, plus Year 4 has an awful lot of writing.

He cried himself to sleep last night, worrying, anxious that his teacher might show the class his work as an example of bad spelling. Other nights, it's because his regular teacher might be away, and a relief teacher might ask him to read out loud or call him lazy when he can't answer a question – that's happened a few times now.

He generally likes school, is thriving in sport, has made good friends and really likes his teacher. He just wishes his reading and writing could be as good as other kids'.

Mattie's an intelligent boy who has severe language and literacy difficulties. He's a gifted athlete and, by nature, he's extremely competitive. His language skills and word-reading are improving steadily, but that's not yet flowed through to his spelling and writing – it will.

Mattie has what I term *Language, Literacy and Learning Disorder* (LLLD): it includes both his Dyslexia (severe literacy learning disability) and Developmental Language Disorder (severely weak language skills).

Mattie also has Attention Deficit/Hyperactivity Disorder (AD/HD).

Despite having these multiple disabilities at a severe level, Mattie doesn't receive any funded disability support at school, or speech language pathology intervention.

Unfortunately, *Learning Disability*, a major disability funding category in the USA, which includes dyslexia dysgraphia and dyscalculia (reading, writing and numeracy difficulties) hasn't been included as a category for school disability funding here. It should be.

Additionally, the criteria that our states use for their communication disability category are very restrictive, quite likely unethically so, by international standards.

Consequently, many kids who have severe communication weakness aren't found eligible for disability funding for their schools. More bunyips.

Thus, Mattie and his school have missed out on funded support despite his severe difficulties. His application for *National Disability Insurance Scheme* (NDIS) funding for speech language pathology and counselling intervention was also rejected – that happens often for kids with no official disability diagnosis (a.k.a. *disability label*). Another bunyip.

Mattie is one of our crushed and crumpled koalas, a sad outcome of Australian education.

He seemed destined for success before he started school. That notion now seems long gone – and this lad is really feeling it.

Three of the 10 Changes emphasise us changing so we meet our teaching challenges for our Matties extremely well.

Change 4 is *One size education does not fit all: Teach to the decidedly different instructional needs of upper-third and lower-third readers*. Let's insist we improve exponentially for our lower-third, in improving education for all our kids.

Change 6 emphasises, *Enrich every child: Ensure effective, supportive, tailored education*. We don't want education that our kids merely tolerate and survive. Let's instead achieve rich education in which they revel and thrive.

If Australian education prioritised those changes, Mattie would have received all the supports he needed, with no need for either a diagnostic label or NDIS funding.

Our Education Act enshrines our kids' needs being met effectively, but currently that seems largely rhetoric, given how badly so many cute koalas miss out.

Change 7 sets a key goal we need to reach. It states, *Insist on easy early-literacy development: Reach regular-orthography nations' achievement levels*. Regular-orthography nations have vastly easier reading and literacy development than we have, to an extent that's currently unthinkable here. That's a very important bunyip.

We too could achieve rapid, easier literacy development, quite easily, for virtually all our cute koalas, if we actioned Change 8: *Investigate the potential of fully-regular beginners' orthographies: Research shows they're key.*

Using a fully-regular English beginners' orthography first, prior to reading and writing Standard English, would make a world of positive difference for our Matties.

In addition, our Matties, and their teachers and schools, desperately need improved school resourcing, so all our cute koalas can receive the rich education they're promised by our Education Act and agreements.

We could then toss out requirements for diagnostic labels for school disability funding, and simply give our kids the highly effective education they're entitled to.

Nathan, Age 9

Nathan has severe speech disorder, with most people finding his speech unintelligible. He also has severe reading and literacy difficulties. Now in Year 4, his literacy skills are at a Year 1 level, and he's struggling socially because it's so hard to communicate effectively with others.

Nathan's speech difficulties are vastly more severe than those of most kids with speech disorder. He has needed government-funded, intensive, ongoing intervention from when he was three or four, working frequently, one-on-one, with a speech language pathologist.

But he's never received it.

As a pre-schooler, he spent 18 months on a waiting list for Community Health, then started group intervention sessions there. While likely helpful for some kids, group sessions in no way met Nathan's needs for intensive one-on-one intervention.

The number of speech language pathologists in our state schools is woefully inadequate, so considerable time passed before Nathan was seen at school. Sadly, once again, the one-on-one intervention he needed wasn't possible, as school speech language pathologies have a huge workload, each servicing multiple schools with long lists of kids in need.

Instead, a speech program was provided in a scrapbook, to be practised at school with teacher aides. Not surprisingly, this also failed to effectively meet his needs.

Thus Nathan is in Year 4 with severe speech difficulties that should have been resolved years ago, but haven't been, because he's never been provided with the supports he needed. Plus, he now has extremely severe reading and learning struggles, and appreciable socialising difficulties.

Nathan's family sought private support from me, but being far from wealthy, could only afford occasional sessions. Thus, once again, there's been not enough intervention to fully meet Nathan's needs. While making progress, he still has major needs.

At school, he wasn't found eligible for government-funded support on the basis of his communication difficulties. Ironically, despite his incredibly severe speech difficulties, he was deemed ineligible because his language scores were above the state's extremely low cut-off criteria. His NDIS application was also denied.

Nathan is yet another crushed and crumpled koala, a victim of the inadequate supports too many Aussie kids experience.

It's appalling, really, that we have only a semblance of free allied-health services for our kids. We need to change that.

Given the emphatic promises of our Education Act, ample, free occupational therapy and speech language pathology services should be a reality here, available to all Aussie kids from birth to 18 years.

Multiple other documents similarly decree that our kids' learning needs should be amply supported:
- Our education systems' disability documents.
- The United Nations Convention on the Rights of the Child and Convention on the Rights of Persons with Disabilities to which Australia is signatory.
- The Alice Springs (Mparntwe) Education Declaration.

Alas, our current reality is a sad lack of services. All too often, kids' serious difficulties aren't sufficiently supported. That's a very sad bunyip.

While Nathan's speech difficulties were obvious to all, his areas of weak language skills lay largely hidden. So did the extent of his severe word-reading difficulties.

That's because our national testing and most schools don't routinely assess language skills and word-reading, so kids' specific needs often aren't obvious, and can be overlooked.

Change 5 states, *End our data deficiency: Build strong knowledge on word-reading levels*. It's much needed.

Change 6, *Enrich every child: Ensure effective, supportive, tailored education*, implies similar needs to monitor kids' language-skills development, as part of enriching learning.

They would make a massive difference for our Nathans.

Jamie, Age 7

Jamie is extremely distractible and struggles to focus on word-reading. He reads the word *bus* and his mind quickly tangents away – now he's talking bus engines.

A clever boy with autism, Jamie had good potential for hyperlexia – word-reading and spelling skills being healthy and well above his weak language reasoning skills. Hyperlexia is common in kids with traits of autism. But for Jamie, anxiety crowded it out. With him now skittish and work-avoidant, it will take time till he's progressing well.

As part of his autistic traits, Jamie lives with anxiety and sensory confusion. Having marked attention deficit traits, his mind flicks quickly to other ideas, so he's easily lost and left behind. Combining these with major dyslexic traits, at school Jamie urgently needed gentle, effective building of readiness for literacy learning, then skilful, carefully-supported word-reading instruction.

Success is crucial for our at-risk joeys. They need ample, ongoing, carefully-tailored, intensive teaching and supports to keep them firmly on the path to success. This builds literacy skills plus confidence and self-esteem, along with the resilience kids need to persist when learning is trickier.

With school resourcing so low, and remedial supports too few, Jamie didn't get tailored instruction matched to his needs. This bright, destined-for-success, wee koala kid is crushed and crumpled now.

Jamie will need extensive intervention before he's back on the path to success and feeling confident. It would have been so much kinder to have kept him there from the start.

Change 2 states, *Own our struggling reader woes: End hypocrisy and pretence.*

We've far too many Matties, Nathans and Jamies in our schools. It's time to take ownership of the inadequate supports and services that too many crushed and crumpled koala kids are experiencing.

Change is needed, highly effective change, that's for sure.

Wendy

Wendy is a high-school learning-support teacher of many years' experience, with whom I taught some years ago. We've been trying to catch up for a get-together.

It's proving difficult – we've already rescheduled three times. First, it was teacher professional development fitted in after school. Next, it was individualised learning plans, far too much work for school hours, thus working nights.

Teaching is time-consuming, and Wendy works days, nights, weekends, and holidays. Her own children are now away at university but, as many friends attest, the time that used to be family time now goes into schoolwork.

The end goals of education haven't changed – some kids off to university, others into apprenticeships, and so on. But you'd never guess that from the relentless pressure our teachers endure.

Teacher administration and paperwork has increased exponentially this century. Additionally, as is the case with most Queensland schools, Wendy's school is implementing multiple teaching improvement initiatives, which further increase teacher busyness.

Wendy is thus extremely busy. The time that should be Wendy-time is instead usually work-time, consumed by the ever increasing demands of our education system, that vortex of chaotic urgency.

It's easiest to catch up during school holidays – she does schoolwork then too, but get-togethers can be prioritised.

A friend of mine, a counsellor, commented that counsellors now work more with teachers than any other profession. I'm not surprised – too many of our teachers are crushed and crumpled too.

We work them far too hard, with unrealistic expectations and unattainable goals. They work far harder than teachers in most nations. We must change that.

Our kids too have woefully high workload, and this in turn adds to teacher busyness. Our schools live with their ubiquitous *Find the Learning Time Challenge* and also their similarly ubiquitous *Find the Caring Time Challenge*. These are very much a workload issue.

Change 3 is *Weigh workload: Our children and teachers are working far too hard*. We need to seriously examine the excessive workloads our kids and teachers endure.

Our Sad Bad Early Years Factory

Reading is life ... Ministers say, in defending what is defensible in many ways but indefensible in others, yes, we're doing extremely well. Everything's terrific. But what those figures hide is about thirty per cent of Australian children who are leaving the school system in Australia are functionally illiterate ... Reading is life!

Brendan Nelson, Federal Minister for Education[ix], 2005

Australian education is struggling badly. It's ineffective in key areas, immensely so.

This is easily evident – just visit schools, observe in classrooms, and peruse work samples of weaker readers.

It's equally apparent in our low results in international *Program for International Student Assessment* (PISA) studies of our high-schoolers' Reading, Science and Maths achievement; and in our too many weak primary-school readers in international *Progress in International Reading Literacy Study* (PIRLS) studies.

The basis of our education woes lies in how ineffective our early-years instruction is for too many vulnerable cute koala joeys. (It's not only kangaroos that have joeys – all our marsupials do. Our joeys in this book are our littlies in Prep and Year 1 – our beginning readers.)

The *Early Years Factory* is the term I use for Australian education for the first three years of formal schooling, from

Foundation year, or Prep (as it's called in Queensland, Tasmania and Victoria), through Year 2. The factory produces our ongoing flood of struggling readers. Our happy, confident koalas seem destined for success at start of school, but by Year 3, our lower-third of readers and learners are now crushed and crumpled koalas, with our middle-third somewhat cranky and crestfallen to boot. It's an ongoing, seemingly endless flood of struggling readers, with more crushed and crumpled koalas added every year.

My snapshot kids, Mattie, Nathan and Jamie are classic products of our Early Years Factory. They were at-risk, and we failed to meet our teaching challenges. Their struggles epitomise our Find the Learning Time Challenge, our Find the Caring Time Challenge, and our education woes.

For beginning readers, word-reading is all too often the area where reading and literacy difficulties commence.

Word-reading is the ability to read words: familiar words, unfamiliar words and also word-parts, e.g. letter-groups and syllables. *Unfamiliar words* are words that are unfamiliar for word-reading. They're often highly familiar spoken words, e.g., *why, eight, pterodactyl, sure, splash*, but when kids encounter them in reading, they're not familiar words they recognise immediately and read easily. Instead, kids have to work them out, i.e., decode them.

Word-reading of unfamiliar words is a particular challenge for Standard English readers. That's a bunyip. Studies that *The Research Tours* explores show the very major struggles that kids experience with reading unfamiliar words.

Kids develop Standard English word-reading difficulties, irrespective of their intelligence and ability levels. Most commonly, weak word-readers have a family history of reading or spelling difficulties, and also weak cognitive-processing and expressive-language skills.

While starting with word-reading difficulties, kids' literacy difficulties then proliferate, soon including struggles with reading, spelling, writing, understanding what they read, and expressing their thoughts effectively in writing. Many struggling readers also develop self-esteem difficulties, and some develop social and behaviour difficulties as well.

That seems enough, doesn't it – but wait, there's more! Because reading and writing are relied on in subject-area learning, e.g., Science and History, kids also struggle there.

For all too many crushed and crumpled cute koalas, their problems continue across the school years. Just ask high-school teachers about the weak reading, learning and assignment skills of their many struggling readers. Ask too about the low confidence and engagement so many have.

Many lower-third readers and learners, our struggling readers, will join our *Spelling Generations*, our generations of kids and adults with sadly insufficient literacy skills, who experience major disadvantages across life.

Let's declare an end to our Spelling Generations.

We can, you know.

South Korea did, and so did Taiwan, Japan and China. They achieved it, quite easily, by making early-literacy development vastly easier and faster for all their kids.

We could do that too.

Of Thirds and Struggling Readers

Let's focus on improving education thoroughly for all three thirds of our kids.

Pardon me casually discussing our precious children as koalas, kids and thirds, e.g., as lower, middle and upper-third readers. I'm writing using the terms I use when speaking, thus at times it's kids, Aussies and thirds.

Thirds is a useful way to consider our children and their instructional needs. Thirds are also useful for considering teaching needs.

They're for thinking Australia-wide, not on specific schools and classes. Some high-achieving schools might have only a tenth of their kids in Australia's lower-third, and half their kids in the upper-third. In lower-achieving schools, the reverse might well be the case.

In discussing thirds, please may I emphasise that the terms are relative and should never define an individual child, now or ever. My snapshot kids and other struggling readers almost invariably have strengths, not just weaknesses.

Many kids with major reading and writing difficulties have the dyslexic contrast of high visual-spatial and gross-motor coordination skills vs very weak phonological, verbal and literacy skills. They excel at sports, Science, Art, Drama, Computing and so on, and show contrasts of upper and lower-third within the one child. I've worked with countless lower-third struggling readers who are upper-third artists, computer gurus, mechanics, dancers and sports champions.

Importantly, having learning difficulties does not mean kids have low intelligence. Most of our lower-third readers have healthy intelligence, with some quite gifted. And virtually all seemed destined for success, till the Early Years Factory took hold, and learning to read began.

It will almost always be reading and academic learning I'll discuss using thirds, not achievement across all school and life areas. Sometimes thirds relate to specific skills, e.g., I'll discuss lower-third word-readers and spellers – kids who struggle with accurately reading words and accurately spelling the words they're writing.

I'll also often term lower-third readers, *struggling readers*. It's a catch-all term encompassing *struggling word-readers, spellers, readers, writers and learners.*

Thirds are also useful for thinking on schools' resourcing needs and teacher workload. In our schools, in addition to skilful teaching of all academic content, we need every class teacher to simultaneously be

- A motivating coach for the gifted and talented, our upper-third.
- A strong and supportive teacher of average students, our middle-third.

- A strategic remedial specialist for our at-risk and struggling readers, our lower-third.

This means, of course, that all Aussie schools need to be resourced appropriately, so this tailored teaching can be achieved efficiently and effectively.

Developing Vs Struggling Readers

It's useful to make a distinction between our *Developing Readers* and our *Struggling Readers*.

Developing readers are our primary-school kids who, as part of making healthy progress, nonetheless still have relatively fledgling word-reading, spelling, and reading and writing skills. In contrast, our struggling readers read and write poorly relative to their healthy-progress classmates, and need catch-up intervention.

My snapshot kids are struggling readers, achieving far below year-level, with their reading and writing similar to that of much younger developing readers.

The contrast between developing and struggling readers is one of confidence as well as skill. While they might read at similar levels, developing readers tend to feel good about themselves, while struggling readers often feel dreadful.

For our struggling readers, SCHOOL is all too often an acronym for *Sad Cruel Hours of Our Lives*.

We need to close our Early Years Factory, and make our schools great, moving from sad cruel hours to spectacularly cool hours, instead.

Let's end the insufficient effectiveness and sad outcomes of too many cute koalas' first three years of school education. They profoundly influence how successful the kids will be across later school years and in adult life.

The Long Hard Work of Remediating Word-Reading

If you've not had close involvement with struggling readers, learning to read and write can seem a simple matter.

You might then assume that helping struggling readers overcome word-reading and literacy learning difficulties should also be a simple matter.

It's not.

Having worked extensively with children with word-reading and literacy difficulties, may I state categorically that all too often it is no easy task to keep our at-risk beginners on the path to strong success. Once kids' learning difficulties are entrenched, the work is harder still. That's perhaps a bunyip for quite a few of us.

It's especially difficult to rescue our weakest word-readers, in particular our vulnerable lowest-tenth, who often have extremely high intervention needs across all school years.

It's unfortunately not simply an issue of improving our teaching skills and increasing resourcing. As *The Research Tours* explores, it's the complex word-reading and spelling difficulties that using solely Standard English creates.

If our schools were far better resourced, we'd then see somewhat improved results, with perhaps only a tenth of our kids being seriously struggling word-readers, instead of our current third and more.

Unfortunately, that lowest-tenth, our kids with severest word-reading struggles, would still prove our undoing. Many severely weak Standard English readers continue to struggle badly, despite receiving intensive, expert, well-tailored instruction. This suggests that we won't achieve the healthy word-reading, spelling and literacy progress that we need, in at least one tenth of our kids, even with ample time and resourcing.

It really is no mean feat to rescue kids once their word-reading and literacy difficulties are entrenched: to progress them to healthy reading, writing and literacy, then to keep them achieving at healthy levels.

We need to resolve our kids' difficulties earlier, meeting our teaching challenges largely by preventing difficulties from starting. We can do that, using 10 Changes improvements.

The Massive Differences Orthographies Make

A transparent orthography treats even a phonologically immature reader in a lenient manner. It helps in explicating the alphabetic principle, the correspondence between spoken and written language ...
It does not burden the beginning reader with a plethora of correspondence rules; and together with systematic phonics teaching it provides the beginning reader with a simple tool for successful word recognition.

Mikko Aro[x], 2004

English appears to have been based, at least in part, on an etymological principle ...
However, the resulting orthography is not a result of the careful application of this and other principles, but a pastiche of different tendencies at different time periods, with chaos a constant companion.

Richard Venezky[xi], 2004

Change 1 states, *Understand how orthographies matter: English spelling is dragging us down.* Too many Aussies are unaware of just how savage the impacts of English orthographic complexity are on our at-risk kids and on education generally. That's a very important bunyip.

Orthographies are spelling systems, and nations get to choose the orthographies their kids and adults will use. We've chosen to use Standard Australian English. In your computer Spellcheck, you'll see other Standard English orthographies, e.g., UK and US Standard English.

We've also chosen not to initially use a fully-regular beginners' orthography prior to Standard English, to expedite both our kids' early-literacy development, and then their mastering of Standard English.

In discussing orthographies, the term *Grapheme: Phoneme Correspondences* (GPCs) is often used. Graphemes are the letters and letter groups of written words, while phonemes are the sounds of spoken words.

GPCs show the ratio of the numbers of graphemes and phonemes in words' spelling patterns. They can show how many graphemes are used to write an individual sound (phoneme), how many phonemes are represented by an individual spelling pattern (grapheme), and so on.

Our Orthography's Excessively Complex GPCs

Most nations are regular-orthography nations. Their regular orthographies almost exclusively use one-to-one GPCs, with

- A single letter for each sound.
- Each sound written with just its one letter.
- Few spelling patterns beyond common letter-sounds.

Because of this, once kids have learned their letter-sounds, they can soon read and write virtually all words.

Our Standard English orthography is vastly different. It uses the 26 letters of our alphabet to write our 40+ common sounds, using well over 500 spelling patterns.

It is one of the world's exceedingly complex orthographies. Researchers often term regular orthographies *transparent*, because reading and writing are so easy, and kids are soon well in control of all words.

In contrast, they term Standard English *opaque*.

Standard English has masses of overlapping GPCs, with approximately a fifth of words from somewhat irregular to extremely so. This creates much orthographic confusion for our joeys and struggling readers.

Most of our overlapping GPCs are for our 20 common vowel sounds, which we write in a myriad of ways.

For a start, we've one-to-many GPCs. When we read words with the naivety of our beginning readers, who try to read words by using their single letter-sounds, we find that, e.g.,

- Letter P is used, alone and with other letters, for at least five phonemes, as in *pot, photo, pterodactyl, psyche, pneumonia*. Using GPC ratios, we might say it has a 1:5 GPC, 1 grapheme: 5 phonemes.
- Letter O might be considered a 1:11 GPC, being used, singly and in combination, for 11 sounds, as in *ox, go, or, now, to/too, book, boy, come, word, women, today*.

We've a plethora of those one-to-many GPCs.

Then, reversing the order, we've also a profusion of many-to-one GPCs, e.g.,

- The sound of SH has at least a 7:1 GPC, written with at least seven different spellings (graphemes), as in *shoe, nation, mission, social, chef, sugar, schwa*.
- The sound of OR has at least a 14:1 GPC, being written with at least 14 different graphemes, as in *for, sore, roar, pour, source, raw, awe, bought, taught, taut, sauce, talk, war, sure*.

It's when our one-to-many and many-to-one GPCs overlap each other that orthographic complexity gets out of hand. We've a multitude of *many-to-many* or *overlapping GPCs*.

Let's use letter *A* as an example. It's in over 20 graphemes, used for at least 15 vowel phonemes. From the perspective of a naïve reader, it's at least a 20:14 GPC, e.g., in *at / gate, wait, later, gauge, ray, great, gaol, praise, straight / any, said, says, dead / sea / aisle, aye / was / beau, goal, faux, mauve / assault / beauty / ha, ah, ask, far, are, half, laugh, draught / air, dare, bear / naughty, ball, war, saw, author, sauce / heard / hear / ago, mountain, regular*.

Things certainly aren't as simple and delightfully regular as they are in regular orthographies, that's for sure. Virtually every one of our letters is used in many different ways, and virtually every sound has multiple spellings.

Indeed, we've very few one-to-one GPCs used frequently in words our kids encounter. As an example, letter *D* uses its common single sound in most words, e.g., *dog*, but it isn't free of orthographic confusion, as it can be considered a silent letter or to say *J,* as in, e.g., *bridge, hedge, dodge*.

For our beginning readers, our lack of one-to-one GPCs is, in many ways, our downfall – and why English spelling drags our kids, our teachers, and education generally, down in so many ways.

Our Beginners Have Too Much To Think On

Our beginning readers and writers have lots to think about. They're inundated with the confusion that is English orthographic complexity. It creates highly complex learning and ongoing high cognitive load across the years kids are learning to read and write.

This makes both word-reading and spelling development extremely slow and drawn-out, and many at-risk children move into word-reading, spelling and literacy difficulties.

It also makes subject-area learning in our early school years similarly slow and drawn-out, impeded in nasty ways by our cute koala kids' snail-speed early-literacy development.

As we Aussies become increasingly aware of orthographic complexity's nasty impacts, we'll become increasingly ripe for achieving effective change.

Standard English orthographies are among the world's most complex. As Finland's Mikko Aro[xii] (2004) says,

> Studies investigating the effect of orthographic consistency have done so usually in comparison with the extreme, namely English.
> The 'transparency' of an orthography can be best thought of as a continuum.

> *Whereas we might remain uncertain where on this continuum each orthography is objectively located, we can be certain of the extreme positions ...*
> *English is one of the most irregular alphabetic orthographies, and Finnish is certainly one of the most regular.*

It's interesting how, in Anglophone nations, we take pride in spelling competitions. There are no such contests in regular-orthography nations – because regular-orthography kids so quickly become expert spellers and word-readers.

Is that a bunyip for you, our spelling system being so utterly complex relative to other nations' orthographies?

It was for me.

My first and biggest bunyip was realising that our complex English spelling was a big answer to my three wonderings:
- What factors cause our kids and adults' reading and literacy difficulties?
- How can we reduce their struggles and suffering?
- What are the ways we can do things better?

Clearly, poorly managed English orthographic complexity is a major factor causing our failure to meet our teaching challenges, and our reading and literacy difficulties.

You may have noticed I'm not advocating spelling reform. That's not a priority of mine. My priority is easing early-literacy development, school life and education.

That said, it's useful to acknowledge that we've allowed Standard English spelling to control us, rather than us controlling it, as regular-orthography nations do. In doing so, we've made a massive rod for our backs, in terms of the workload and time needed for us to build word-reading and spelling skills. While regular-orthography nations control spelling, Standard English spelling controls us.

We've let spelling be overly difficult and time-consuming, e.g., we've not sufficiently controlled when consonants are single or double in multisyllabic words, so kids often have to learn each word – that's hundreds of learning hours.

We've also allowed over 20 spellings for the *schwa* (ə), our commonest vowel sound – more hundreds of teaching and learning hours. Our lack of awareness of the schwa is a sad bunyip: it's amazing how many of us don't know of it.

Sounding somewhat like ŭ as in *us*, the schwa abounds in words, in unstressed syllables. Note its different spellings in *plat<u>y</u>pus, moth<u>er</u>, maj<u>or</u>, b<u>e</u>gin, wom<u>a</u>n, wom<u>e</u>n, mount<u>ai</u>n, vir<u>us</u>, Dav<u>i</u>d, pri<u>sm</u>/pris<u>o</u>n, pan<u>el</u>/litt<u>le</u>/fin<u>al</u>/speci<u>al</u>*.

We have masses of homographs (identically written words with different pronunciations), which kids must negotiate, e.g., "I'll *lead* as we *desert* you in this *lead* hot *desert*"; and a myriad of homophones (identically pronounced words with different spellings), e.g., *ate/eight, or/awe, for/four, I/eye, right/write, meet/meat, weak/week, practice/practise*.

This orthographic confusion greatly increases the teaching and learning time kids need. Just ask teachers how much time they spend correcting *who/how, there/their/they're, where/we're/wear/were, whose/who's, its/it's,* and endings such as *-able/-ible, -ance/-ence, -tion/-sion* – they're a veritable black hole of teaching and learning hours.

For reading, our beginning readers struggle with uncertain pronunciation because our graphemes can be pronounced so many different ways.

Because of our overlapping GPCs, particularly our vowel graphemes having many phoneme options, most unfamiliar words that our kids meet have ambiguous pronunciation.

As a country kid and avid reader, I knew precisely what a chauffeur was, but pronounced it *choffer* till I hit the city lights. I'm also perhaps not the only Harry Potter fan who mispronounced Hermione as *Her-me-own* till the first Harry Potter movie came out.

Uncertain pronunciation is a much lesser issue for regular-orthography nations, as their spelling often shows words' pronunciation far more consistently.

This makes reading simpler and easier, with kids quickly becoming confident, independent readers and writers.

Certainly, orthographic complexity and its impacts, and particularly our kids' difficulties reading unfamiliar words, underlie many of our education woes.

The Research Tours explores the findings of pertinent studies that show the challenges we make for ourselves, when we launch our joeys directly into English orthographic complexity's whirl of confusion. In addition, Book 3 of the *Aussie Reading Woes* trilogy, *The 10 Changes: The Nitty Gritty* includes considerable facts and detail on orthographic complexity and its many impacts.

The Joys of Regular Orthographies

While the Anglosphere wrestles with massive orthographic complexity, the world's many regular-orthography nations enjoy simple learning across early-literacy development.

Some use extremely regular orthographies, with less than 50 GPCs, e.g., Finnish, Estonian, Polish, Spanish, Italian and Greek. They've only a tiny amount of learning, mostly just letter-sounds, and kids master word-reading and spelling in weeks to months. There are a few bunyips lurking here.

In nations with the most regular orthographies, e.g., Finland, while it takes a few years to achieve adult speed, most kids can accurately read and write all the words that adults can, before the end of Grade 1.

Because learning to read and write regular orthographies is so straightforward and easy,
- Kids are very soon confident, independent readers and writers, within a single school year.
- Few kids have word-reading and spelling difficulties, and their difficulties are minor.
- Early intervention works extremely well, even for kids with significant intellectual disability, because learning to read and write has such simple learning.
- Subject-area learning is expedited because kids are confident, literate learners.

I find myself green with envy when Finnish researchers discuss the majority of Finnish children reading with adult accuracy by mid-Grade 1, and errors being quite rare after Grade 1, even in less-fluent readers.

In comparison, word-reading and spelling development here are inordinately prolonged. Our test norms show our kids take at least six and nine years, on average, to reach reasonably-skilled word-reading and spelling accuracy, still well below expert-adult level. That's also *on average*, with hordes taking far longer, and many never being proficient.

Orthographic confusion impedes our koala joeys' learning, immensely slowing word-reading and spelling development.

Is that a bunyip for you, the fact that in many nations, kids have proficiently-accurate word-reading and spelling in less than a year, while our kids take at least six to nine years?

Another bunyip is the massive spread of word-reading and spelling achievement we have in each year-level, which complicates teaching and learning in major ways. Regular-orthography nations don't have that, as, while reading speed might vary, virtually all kids are confident, accurate readers and writers by Grade 2.

Aussie teachers, wouldn't you just love that?

Their kids are all on the same playing field, while that's not the case for our weaker word-readers. Very large numbers of our kids steadily fall behind, one paddock, two paddocks, three paddocks, four, away from their year-level playing field. Those wide skill differences add hugely to teachers' workload. That's another bunyip.

We've massive differences between stronger and weaker word-readers – that gap is a major disadvantage, one that regular-orthography nations don't have.

While, by regular-orthography standards, our upper-third and some of our middle-third word-readers are hugely slow developers, they do well by Anglophone standards. But our lower-third trail far behind.

Then, one more very sad bunyip: our crushed and crumpled struggling word-readers, which our Early Years Factory has savagely mauled.

Regular-orthography nations have few struggling word-readers and spellers, with their difficulties quite minor. In contrast, just as an animal's tail drags behind it, in our reading and learning distribution, we've a long sad tail of underachievers with serious reading struggles.

They lag far behind their healthy-progress peers – and a world away from regular-orthography weaker readers.

The Research Tours explores interesting studies showing us the challenges of Standard English word-reading and spelling, and our long sad tail of struggling readers.

We've indeed a crowd of bunyips in our classrooms.

It's Bikes Vs Trucks

From practical perspectives, regular-orthography word-reading and spelling are easily acquired skills, somewhat akin to learning to swim or ride a bike.

Kids quickly move from *I can't* to *I can*, often experiencing a sequence of *I can't do it! ... Oh, now I can ... Wow, look at me now, I'm amazing!* with a delighted *Aha* moment of wonder, amazement and pride at having mastered this seemingly elusive skill.

Our CQU research team, Professor Bruce Knight, myself and other colleagues, have likened learning to read and write fully-regular orthographies to learning to ride a bike in ideal conditions – on a smooth path amidst delightful weather and wonderfully supportive company. We included that analogy in the title of our 2013 research journal article, *Because trucks aren't bicycles: Orthographic complexity as a disregarded variable in reading research.*

And in the same way that few of us need remedial lessons for bike riding or swimming, very few regular-orthography children need word-reading and spelling remediation.

For those kids who do experience delay, compared to our kids' struggles, their difficulties are minute. Because of this, intervention in regular-orthography nations works very well, with delayed learners soon proficiently accurate.

Our team likened learning to read and write Standard English to learning to drive an all-terrain vehicle, a truck, in confusing, oft-changing circumstances, off-road in nasty weather. It's difficult complex learning that demands careful teaching and copious practice – so is learning to read and write Standard English.

Change 7 is *Insist on easier early-literacy development: Reach regular-orthography nations' achievement levels.* It's a key change that will be massive kindness to our kids, teachers, schools, workforce and nation.

Early-literacy development being so quickly and easily acquired in the world's many regular-orthography nations creates a strong argument that ethically our kids are entitled to similar ease.

We're supposed to be the *Lucky Country*, after all.

At present it might seem a big ask. It's not, particularly if we also take on Changes 8 and 9:
- Change 8: Investigate the potential of beginners' orthographies: Research shows they're key.
- Change 9: First, play to learn: Start Standard English word-reading instruction from mid-Year 2.

The Trials of Standard English Orthography

Learning to read and write is exponentially more difficult for our kids, because English orthographic complexity slows and complicates word-reading and spelling development.

Our koala joeys too often meet our 20 common vowel-sounds spelled different ways, plus new graphemes that are initially confusing, e.g., *ou, our, ph, ew, ough, all, au, ey, igh, -tion*.

Importantly, many of our most frequent words have highly irregular spelling. That's why we teach our kids whole-word sightwords. This can usefully supplement schools' teaching of sounding-out of regular words.

Just notice the different pronunciations of the underlined graphemes in these words: w<u>a</u>s/h<u>a</u>s, th<u>ey</u>/k<u>ey</u>, wh<u>at</u>/wh<u>o</u>, <u>one</u>/d<u>one</u>/b<u>one</u>, n<u>igh</u>t/<u>eigh</u>t, h<u>ere</u>/w<u>ere</u>, s<u>ome</u>/h<u>ome</u>.

Because these words are seen so often, their contrasting GPCs cause greater confusion for our cute koala joeys. Because virtually all words in regular-orthography nations are regular, their kids have little to none of this confusion.

The good news is that the majority of our words and syllables are regular and can be sounded out. The bad news is that our beginners meet a plethora of less-regular unfamiliar words, for which sounding-out doesn't work. Just try pronouncing these words using commonest letter-sounds: *T-h-e t-w-o b-o-y-s w-e-r-e h-e-r-e l-a-s-t n-i-g-h-t.*

Regular-orthography kids can sound-out all words once they know their letter-sounds. Ours can't. Their massive ease vs our sad, massive complexity is another bunyip, one that's well worth reflecting on.

Imagine the ease if our kids too could read and write every single word they meet by sounding-out! That's the regular-orthography norm – and another bunyip.

Now imagine how confident and skilled our kids would be if they first learned to read and write a fully-regular orthography, and were confident, literate, skilled learners when they then learned to read and write Standard English. They'd win, and so would education and Australia.

It bears thinking on, doesn't it?

We've Too High Cognitive Load

Because our beginners' learning is so complex, ongoing high cognitive load is part and parcel of reading, writing and learning across our early school years. That's because our kids so often have lots to think about when trying to read and write less-regular words that they've not yet mastered.

That too high cognitive load means our kids need strong working memory and executive-function skills, if they're to thrive. That's another bunyip.

Ample working memory is essential for our kids if they're to succeed, but isn't vital for regular-orthography kids. Low working-memory not being the problem it is for our kids is why regular-orthography kids with intellectual disability cope very well with word-reading and writing.

Our too high cognitive load reduces kids' comprehension when they've too much to consider. It also exacerbates our joeys' word-reading and spelling difficulties. More bunyips.

It even exacerbates the reading and writing difficulties of our strong word-readers who have language weakness, and struggle with language comprehension and reasoning.

When they pause to think on word-reading and spelling while reading and writing, this reduces working memory available for comprehension and language reasoning. Alas, kids with language weakness often have quite low working memory, so losing working memory to word-reading and spelling is a problem, heightening the language weakness they experience when they read and write. Another bunyip.

Now for a further, extremely important bunyip, worthy of massive embarrassment – the excessive workload and time-pressure that relentlessly hammers our kids and teachers.

Our kids' long, slow, drawn-out word-reading, spelling and early-literacy development makes our schools vastly busier and far more time-pressured than schools in regular-orthography nations. Our teachers and schools really do live with a chronic Find the Learning Time Challenge and Find the Caring Time Challenge. It's an Anglosphere issue, largely non-existent across regular-orthography nations.

It's an issue of time saved vs time spent – another bunyip. Time is saved in regular-orthography nations because word-reading and spelling development take few hours, and this time can instead be spent on learning enrichment and subject-area learning – and even on Finland and Estonia's 15-minute breaks between lessons, for playing and relaxing.

In contrast, we spend massive teaching and learning hours building word-reading, spelling, and independent reading and writing, and supporting kids with weak literacy skills across the six to nine years our kids take, on average, to reach reasonably-accurate word-reading and spelling.

Regular-orthography schools are thus time-rich and literacy-rich, while our schools are time-poor and literacy-poor. Ouch! We really are WYSYAINing badly if we think that things here are fine.

Please note I'm not saying Standard English word-reading development is inevitably a nightmare. Providing kids with tailored levels of systematic word-reading instruction and lots of enjoyable reading works well for many cute koalas.

What I am saying is that
- Our kids' word-reading and spelling development is incredibly slow relative to non-Anglophone nations.
- Our kids have immature reading and writing skills for many years and this impedes subject-area learning.
- Far more of our kids have word-reading and spelling difficulties than regular-orthography kids.
- Our kids' literacy learning difficulties are vastly more severe than those of regular-orthography kids.
- Relative to regular-orthography nations, we spend far too many hours building word-reading and spelling, and supporting developing and struggling readers.
- Our schools are thus time-poor, with reduced time for subject-area learning and learning enrichment.
- Our excessive, complex, early-literacy learning makes our child and teacher workloads too high.
- Together, these factors massively impede education.

And all of those are nasty byproducts of Standard English and our Early Years Factory. It's bunyips galore, for sure.

Most of the 10 Changes emphasise knowledge-building. That's because we're awash with Swiss-cheese research areas, with massive needs to fill important knowledge gaps.

To bridge the wide crosslinguistic divide between us and regular-orthography nations, it is pivotal that we prioritise efficient research studies, large and small, that can build the knowledge we need.

Orthographic Complexity Can Be Managed Well

When the script is less complex, young children appear to develop word recognition skills with relative ease, even in the absence of sufficient linguistic proficiency.

Esther Geva & Linda Siegel[xiii], 2000

It's not English orthographic complexity in itself that causes our troubles: it's how we manage that complexity for our cute koala joeys who are learning to read and write.

By Taiwanese, Japanese and Chinese standards, we're dreadfully mismanaging that complexity. That's perhaps our most major bunyip – quite a cringeworthy one.

Taiwan, Japan and China have orthographies far more complicated than Standard English, with thousands of intricate characters to be learned. Consequently, in times past, they had far more struggling readers and illiterate adults than we have.

They solved their difficulties, and now meet their teaching challenges brilliantly, by implementing one clever simple change, and now manage their orthographic complexity superbly for their beginning readers.

That change was each nation moving from using just its single labyrinthine orthography (China and Taiwan's Hanzi, and Japan's Kanji), to each adding in a fully-regular orthography used when kids first learn to read and write –

Taiwan's Zhuyin Fuhao (also called BoPoMoPho), Japan's Hiragana and China's Pinyin.

Doing this, these nations protect their beginners from the harmful impacts of their complex orthographies, expedite early-literacy and language development, and empower kids' subsequent learning of their complex orthography.

They ensure blissfully easy early-literacy development via the regular orthography, keeping the complex orthography well away till kids are competently and confidently reading and writing their regular beginners' orthography.

As their kids read and write their fully-regular beginners' orthography, they develop empowered cognitive-processing and executive-function skills. Then, armed with strong literacy and learning skills, they transition smoothly and steadily to reading and writing their complex orthography.

It's interesting, isn't it? Kids actually learn to read and write two orthographies far more easily than they'd master the highly-complex orthography on its own – as long as the first orthography is a highly-regular one. While a few kids do have difficulties mastering that complex orthography, as studies in *The Research Tours* explore, both the number of kids who have difficulties, and the extent of their difficulties, are impressively tiny relative to our woes.

These nations also support kids' transitioning and learning of their complex orthography in easy, impressive ways. They apportion very manageable sets of characters to be learned, to each year-level; and in the texts kids read, they write recently-introduced words in both the regular and complex orthographies.

In Japanese children's texts, for example, beside each new Kanji character is a tiny column of Hiragana letters. If kids can't remember the Kanji character, no interruption is experienced – they simply read the Hiragana word and, at the same time, get useful practice with the Kanji character.

This keeps reading fluent, empowers learning and self-teaching, and massively reduces needs for teacher help.

It also improves comprehension, as reading flows smoothly, not interrupted by pausing for words kids can't easily read.

Interestingly, Japanese Grade 1 classes have 37 children, far more than our 25, and they find this very manageable. That's quite likely because their kids so quickly and easily become confident, independent readers and writers who are also strong self-teachers, needing little teacher support.

Our kids lack that rapidly developed self-teaching and are vastly needier – that's a bunyip too.

There's certainly a vast crosslinguistic gap (cross-national gap) between education here, with our struggles, and the ease of education in regular-orthography nations. We need to bridge that gap.

For a start, with Taiwan, Japan, China and Korea now being regular-orthography nations, there are now very few nations with orthographies as complex as Standard English – another bunyip.

Thai is much harder, and not surprisingly, Thailand also has many struggling readers with severe reading and writing difficulties.

Role Models for Our Future Improvement

Taiwan, Japan and China are powerful role models for our improving education into the future, through the strategic orthography changes they made, and their subsequent massive improvement. They're role models for impressive early-literacy development and education, and also for the impressive economic outcomes they've achieved since then, with their widespread, high literacy levels.

Our mantra for our improvement journey is Jackie French's[xiv] *There are no such things as reading difficulties. There are only teaching challenges.* Taiwan, Japan and China really do epitomise that mantra. They realised how word-reading and early-literacy difficulties were optional, and changed to now managing their teaching challenges exceptionally well.

Research studies show very few struggling word-readers: they're very close to *no such things as reading difficulties.*

Our Anglocentrism promotes WYSYAINing (our chronic *What You See, You Assume Is Normal*), and this brings us down badly. We need to be looking outward, leaving behind our chronic circling of the Anglophone fishbowl, and learning from Taiwan, Japan and China's successes. That's why *A* in our ABCs is *Act locally while looking globally.*

We too could easily manage our too high orthographic complexity extremely effectively, by holding it off initially, with our kids initially learning to read and write a fully-regular English beginners' orthography, and then later transitioning to reading and writing Standard English.

That's why Change 8 is emphatic, *Investigate the potential of beginners' orthographies: Research shows they're key.*

The Initial Teaching Alphabet (ITA)

Importantly, we also have an impressive English regular-orthography role model – the *Initial Teaching Alphabet* (ITA, written then as *i.t.a.*).

A myriad of Anglosphere studies in the 1960s showed ITA to be extremely effective in expediting kids' early-literacy development and hugely reducing both schools' numbers of struggling word-readers and spellers, and the kids' extent of difficulties. The studies also showed children transitioned very easily and successfully to using Standard English.

The ITA findings are very much akin to the successes that regular-orthography nations enjoy now.

In future 10 Changes knowledge-building, it's essential we research regular orthographies. We might use ITA or another English fully-regular beginners' orthography, e.g., perhaps *Fleksispel*, an English beginners' orthography I've developed, which has options of multi-stage transitioning.

There are multiple options to choose from, e.g., over 500 regular-orthographies competed for George Bernard Shaw's prize money for an exemplary English orthography.

Reading and writing a fully-regular English beginners' orthography would build strong literacy and learning skills in virtually all our kids. We'd soon end our ongoing flood of crushed and crumpled koala kids struggling with word-reading and spelling. We'd also soon end our Spelling Generations – because we'd no longer be adding in each year's new crowd of poor struggling joeys.

Our kids too would develop enriched cognitive-processing and executive-function skills that would empower learning and ease transitioning to Standard English.

We'd still have kids with some word-reading and spelling difficulties, but the number of kids and their extent of difficulties would be minute relative to those we have at present. And our weaker word-readers would be confidently literate in many ways.

It's likely their difficulties would be for some spellings, e.g.,
- Relatively infrequent irregular words, e.g., thoroughly, echo, antique, sure, giraffe, beautiful, stationery.
- Single vs double consonants, e.g., *cammel* vs *camel*.
- Schwa spellings in less frequent multisyllabic words, e.g., p<u>u</u>sist<u>i</u>nt, pres<u>u</u>dint, el<u>u</u>ph<u>e</u>nt.
- Confusable endings, such as *-tion/-sion*, *-ant/-ent*, *-able/-ible* e.g., suffi<u>ss</u>i<u>a</u>nt, terr<u>a</u>ble, addi<u>ss</u>ion.
- Combinations of the above, e.g., uksepshin<u>u</u>l, sietust.

Our kids' word-reading accuracy would be both capable and confident, as would their spelling of most words. It's likely their spelling difficulties would not be of a level that would greatly impede their writing. After all, Jackie French, AB Facey, Roald Dahl, Agatha Christie and other writers have written wonderful works despite somewhat weak spelling.

We currently control orthographic complexity as best we can by teaching word-reading and spelling systematically and strategically.

By Anglophone nation standards, this works well for many cute koala kids. By international standards, however, it's woeful, for all our kids, and particularly our crushed and crumpled word-readers.

Our at-risk joeys need ample, ongoing, rewarding word-reading success – and all too often, they miss out on it.

Our current instructional methods are too time-consuming, and not effective enough, relative to the strong effects of initially using a fully-regular beginners' orthography.

Standard English is an incredibly complicated orthography, which massively complicates our kids' word-reading and early-literacy development and struggles. Initially using a fully-regular orthography such as ITA or Fleksispel would transform our education world.

Change 1 is important: *Understand how orthographies matter: English spelling is dragging us down.*

It's a vital priority, given so many Australians are largely unaware of the extent to which English spelling impedes us when we use it on its own without a beginners' orthography.

Change 5 is also a key priority: *End our data deficiency: Build strong knowledge on word-reading levels.*

We need to pursue those changes.

Given that orthographic complexity's impacts are seen most strongly in nations' ease vs difficulty of word-reading development, we urgently need word-reading data. Currently, we've woefully little, as Australia doesn't test word-reading systemically.

Our annual NAPLAN (*National Assessment Program – Literacy and Numeracy*) testing gives us useful data on our kids' reading comprehension, spelling, written expression, punctuation and grammar levels.

However, it provides no clear information on the word-reading and language skills kids need for effective literacy.

We need research establishing how quickly and easily our upper, middle and lower-third word-readers develop word-reading and spelling proficiency, and the methods that best meet their instructional needs.

We similarly need research on kids' language-skill levels.

In building this needed knowledge, it's important that we also action Change 8, *Investigate the potential of beginners' orthographies: Research shows they're key.*

We need to explore the advantages of using beginners' orthographies for our kids, towards
- Easing and speeding word-reading and early-literacy development.
- Reducing both literacy and learning difficulties.
- Reducing the high workload and time-pressure our kids and teachers endure.
- Empowering reading and writing of Standard English.
- Enhancing literacy and language development.
- Increasing the efficiency of subject-area learning.

Our beginners' orthography would quite likely be used solely for the very early stages of reading and writing. That's how Taiwan's BoPoMoPho, China's Pinyin, and the Initial Teaching Alphabet (ITA) are used. In contrast, Japan uses Hiragana first as its beginners' orthography for early-literacy development, then also uses it on an ongoing basis for adults and children, with grammatical-marker words usually being written in Hiragana.

We too would have options of how we'd balance use of our beginners' orthography and Standard English. We'd likely use the beginners' orthography with Standard English in children's books and texts, and signs might say both *Caution! Danger!* and *Corshun! Daenju!* to assist our adult Aussies who have weak word-reading.

Suffice to say, at present, we're not managing Standard English orthographic complexity nearly well enough, and this is inflicting ongoing damage on our cute koala kids, Spelling Generations adults, teachers, education and nation.

Our schools are pressure-cookers, and we can't afford their stress and time-pressure, or the widespread, weak literacy skills of so many Aussie kids and adults.

It's time for 10 Changes improvements, that's for sure.

Our Struggling-Education Problem

If we teach today's students as we taught yesterday's, we rob them of tomorrow.

John Dewey[xv], 1916

We've a complicated problem of education struggling badly, with too little success, and excessive disadvantages and difficulties. It's complex, multifaceted and intractable. We have far too many struggling readers, and we do too poorly relative to far too many other nations.

We're treading water rather than swimming, achieving too little improvement for the enormous efforts our teachers and kids expend.

We've challenges galore, e.g., Geoff Masters (2016) details *Five challenges in Australian school education*:

- Too many learners significantly below year-level.
- One fifth of children being at-risk on school entry, and vulnerable for long-term, low achievement.
- Declining reading and maths achievement.
- Growing disparities between schools that are strongly linked to Socio-Economic Status (SES).
- Teaching no longer being a desirable career option.

Orthographic Advantage Vs Disadvantage

Orthographic Advantage Theory, developed by our CQU team[xvi], is a tool for considering cross-national differences.

> *Orthographic Advantage Theory proposes that, according to their level of orthographic complexity, nations experience disadvantage and potential advantage in multiple areas of education and national functioning [including]*
> *1. Ease of early-literacy development,*
> *2. Simplified school instruction and learning across primary and secondary school,*
> *3. Ease of improving education,*
> *4. Impacts of reduced workplace illiteracy,*
> *5. Increased adult life advantage, and*
> *6. Generational advantage through confidently literate parents being able to effectively support their children's literacy development.*

That's the wide crosslinguistic gap that separates us from the ease of regular-orthography nations. It starts with the level of difficulty kids experience when learning to read and write, and expands from there.

Worlds of Es and Cs

Using Standard English on its own, without a beginners' orthography, we have severe orthographic disadvantage. Our world is a whirl of Cs: we have Confused, Complicated, Chaotic learning, and a Cluttered-Curriculum Conundrum of having too much to teach in too little time. That's because we spend so much time on word-reading and spelling, and supporting kids' weak literacy skills during subject-area learning, while still having to fit in all the subject-area content that children in all nations study.

Regular-orthography nations with a single highly-regular orthography, e.g., Finland and Estonia, are *Easy Education Nations*. Working strategically, they can enjoy very strong orthographic advantage. Many use it to excellent effect.

They live with Es, a.k.a. Ease. They have Easy, Expedited, Efficient, Effective Education that's relatively Effortless too. That's because their schools spend so little time on word-reading and spelling before their kids are highly skilled.

Teaching to confident, independent readers, writers and learners from Grade 2, they're time-rich for other learning.

Our education world is sadly different. We're chronically time-poor, have too much to teach, have far too many weak readers, and virtually all our kids are sadly slow to become confident, independent readers, writers and learners.

Taiwan, Japan and China are *Semi-Easy Education Nations*, as they've the additional workload of mastering a second orthography. Even so, they're miles ahead of us, as their kids are so quickly confident, literate, independent learners. They live with Es too, with little sign of Cs. Now, that's a very important bunyip.

Using Standard English without a beginners' orthography, we're currently stuck with our nasty Cs, in an education whirl we'd love to leave behind. Our teachers and kids wrestle with this vortex of chaotic complexity.

Let's now consider the interacting impacts of three key factors that underlie and contribute to our education difficulties. They're integral to our Early Years Factory:
- Factor 1: Orthographic complexity – the foundations and infrastructure of our Early Years Factory.
- Factor 2: Our kids' young age when learning to read – the factory entrance.
- Factor 3: Insufficient school resourcing – it switches on the factory's conveyor belt.

They're a fearsome trio that work together in nasty ways.

Factor 1: English Orthographic Complexity

Managing English orthographic complexity effectively is currently our biggest teaching challenge. We've inherited one of the world's most complex spelling systems, and we're not managing that complexity nearly well enough for our beginning readers – our cute koala joeys.

In most regular-orthography nations, kids quickly develop proficient word-reading and spelling in their first year of school, and can soon read and write as accurately as adults.

Meanwhile, our kids take six to nine years, on average, to reach what we consider a reasonable level of skill – but it's well below proficient adult-level word-reading and spelling.

On average is an interesting term. Said quickly, we might think almost all kids have strong accuracy levels after six and nine years, but that's far from being the case. We've our long sad tail of underachievers: our lower-third who take far longer, with many never confidently accurate.

They instead join our Spelling Generations. They leave school still struggling, having spent their entire school years as somewhat illiterate, struggling learners. Many of them become parents who, in turn, struggle to support and develop their children's language and literacy readiness.

This doesn't happen in regular-orthography nations, where early intervention is highly effective. Their lower-third and indeed their lowest-tenth word-readers and spellers might be somewhat less fluent, but they're proficiently accurate by Grade 3 or 4: that's long before our healthy-progress kids. Thus, virtually all their high-school graduates are highly literate, and parents can confidently read to their children.

We're thus sadly WYSYAINing when we accept as normal that our poor kids develop word-reading, spelling, and independent reading and writing so very slowly, with so many kids and adults enduring ongoing literacy struggles – all because they were born here in Australia, instead of in Austria, China, Estonia, Finland, Greece, Italy, Japan, Poland, Russia, Taiwan, Turkey, Wales, etc., etc., etc.

Yes, English orthographic complexity contributes in major ways to our education woes. It's the infrastructure, the buildings and machinery of our Early Years Factory, in place, ready to perpetuate our flood of struggling readers.

Factor 2: Too Young Koalas

Aged only 4.5 to 5 years, our joeys are too young for the highly complex learning that's part and parcel of learning to read and write Standard English. That's a sad bunyip.

At that young age, many have far too immature learning skills. While currently it's a Swiss-cheese research area, future research may well establish young age as a major factor in why word-reading and spelling develop so much more slowly here, and why so many kids struggle.

Our joeys being too young is perhaps the entrance to our Early Years Factory. Our wee koala joeys play happily on the path outside, blissfully unaware of sad challenges ahead, till the factory drags them in. Indeed, the families of most of our struggling readers considered them destined for success before they started school and learning to read. And most would have achieved that success, had they been born in a nation that uses a regular-orthography – but here, alas, it's solely Standard English, and the factory drags them in.

Complex learning requires healthy cognitive-processing and executive-function skills. These skills are far weaker at 4.5 to 5 years, and much stronger at 7 to 8 years, when kids in many European regular-orthography nations start school and learn to read and write. That's another bunyip.

Standard English is packed with complex learning, thus our kids need strong cognitive-processing skills. But alas, we start reading far younger than many nations, at an age when many of our joey's cognitive-processing skills are decidedly immature, and this sets them up for learning struggles.

Further, and another bunyip, many potential risk factors stay dormant if children initially learn to read and write a regular-orthography. Starting our at-risk joeys on Standard English at 4.5 to 5 years first activates risk factors, and then proliferates their impacts. This virtually guarantees that many of our cute koala joeys will struggle.

Pressure on schools to increase outcomes has made things worse. Notably, the Australian Curriculum has moved word-reading and spelling instruction down from Year 1 to Prep.

For our at-risk kids, that's a sad and damaging change. It quite likely increases our numbers of struggling readers and the severity of their difficulties. It may well underlie our increasing numbers of PIRLS and PISA low achievers.

Importantly, it takes a lot longer to teach complex content when children are very young. Spending so much time on reading and early literacy, our schools then run short on time for subject-area learning, play-based learning and play generally – hence we also produce dispirited learners. More bunyips, for sure.

By starting word-reading instruction at age 4.5 to 5 years, we're forcing our joeys to grow up too quickly and harshly, demanding they master highly complex learning that many aren't capable of, and stealing their time for play.

The inefficiency of our starting learning so young is obvious when we consider a further bunyip: our kids doing 300 more hours of schooling each year than kids in many regular-orthography nations, as OECD studies show.

Our making such small gains despite such long hours highlights both how inefficient education is here, and how inappropriate it is to work our kids so hard when so young.

We wouldn't insist our Prep joeys master the two-times-tables, fractions and numbers to a million in their first year of schooling. We'd recognise that as developmentally inappropriate, knowing they'll do that learning vastly more effectively when older, with more mature learning skills.

However, we unthinkingly demand mastery of far more complex learning through insisting they make impressive progress with Standard English.

Is that another bunyip? It's certainly classic WYSYAIN. Starting at age 4.5 to 5 years, rather than at age 7, when many European kids learn to read and write, might seem normal – but only in Anglophone nations. By the standards of regular-orthography nations, starting so young is not just inefficient – it's also illogical and somewhat cruel.

Change 9 is *First, play to learn: Start Standard English word-reading instruction from mid-Year 2*. Actioning this key change effectively, we'd improve education for all our kids, and could build a surge of enthusiastic learners.

Factor 3: Inadequate School Resourcing

The poor resourcing our schools have for word-reading and early-literacy instruction across Early Years Factory years equates to *Power on, all systems go!* When word-reading instruction starts, the conveyor belt switches on, and off our kids go, with about one in three soon offloaded from destined-for-success to life-of-struggles.

Fortunately, although they're well behind kids in regular-orthography nations, most of our upper and middle-third kids leave the factory as confident, relatively successful readers and writers, thanks to our teachers' efforts.

But alas, the low resourcing we provide for our kids' highly complex learning has our lower-third emerging as crushed and crumpled, sadly resigned, cute koala kids. Many remain struggling readers, joining our Spelling Generations.

We're not resourcing our schools sufficiently or efficiently for all three thirds of kids. In our early years, given our kids are wrestling with Standard English, our usual adult: child ratio of one teacher to 25 cute koalas is inappropriately severe. It almost guarantees we won't meet our teaching challenges for many cute koalas, especially lower-third readers. Combining English orthographic complexity and too young kids with too low resourcing is a disastrous combination.

Add to this our kids and teachers' much higher workloads, and it's obvious our adult: child ratio needs to be adjusted, to perhaps one adult to 10 children from Prep to Year 2 for both literacy lessons and subject-area learning that involves reading and writing.

We've far too few teachers and teacher aides. We've also far too few learning-support teachers, learning-support aides, speech language pathologists, occupational therapists, and allied-health aides.

We underinvest in early-literacy development to our peril, as doing so overinvests in our struggles. Our school resourcing is no larger than that of Finland, yet our support needs are vastly higher, due to learning to read and write being so much more complex, and our kids being very young.

Schools in nations such as Finland and Estonia need only quite minimal supports. Their Grade 1 kids are 7 to 8 years old, and thus have strong cognitive-processing and learning skills. Further, learning to read and write highly-regular Finnish and Estonian is so easy that more than half their kids are reading when they start Grade 1, and virtually all are confident, independent readers and writers by Grade 2.

Given our kids are so young, and must do exponentially harder learning, our early-years classroom and learning-support resourcing should be vastly higher. But it's not.

That's one reason our teachers spend so much of their own money on resourcing. It's common to hear teachers setting an annual budget of $1,000 or $2,000 of their personal funds for school needs, and they too easily spend far more.

Resourcing is not a specific 10 Changes target. Increased resourcing is simply a given, till education here is achieving as well as schools routinely achieve across nations such as Taiwan, Japan and China.

Our so heavily restricting our resourcing for our early-years instruction and intervention means we've been paying the high costs of orthographic disadvantage in the struggles of our lower-third readers and overworked teachers.

That's not appropriate. It's now time to pay those costs in increased school resourcing and research.

Let's face it, we've inadvertently chosen an inordinately expensive spelling system. Bunyips, anyone?

Strategic, effective change is going to involve considerable resourcing and much higher expense, until we've achieved the impressive improvements that we're due.

It's then we'll achieve long-term savings.

Our Factory's Nasty Byproducts

Most factories produce prioritised products, and also less-desirable byproducts. Our Early Years Factory produces at least 10 byproducts that impede education in nasty ways.

It produces Nasty Byproduct 1: the too slow word-reading and spelling development of all our cute koalas.

It also produces Nasty Byproduct 2: the suffering and struggles of our weak readers of all ages, that commence in their factory years.

It also creates Nasty Byproduct 3: the much less effective learning our developing and struggling readers do across all subject areas, because of their still-fledgling reading and writing skills.

This byproduct too has insidious effects. Let's consider learning efficiency: our koalas' less efficient learning vs the far stronger learning of regular-orthography children.

Let's think on how much learning Grade 2 Estonian (regular-orthography) children might do in, e.g. History, Science and Geography, and compare it with our Year 2 kids' learning. The two groups will have had the same amount of formal schooling, now being in their third school year.

It's Swiss-cheese research time, but there's every likelihood that the Estonian kids would achieve far more sophisticated learning. They're 8 to 9 years old and highly literate, whereas our Year 2 kids are 6 to 7 years old and fledgling readers and writers, who still need lots of help when reading and writing during subject-area learning.

It seems a useful research area, doesn't it?

We'd consider, and then explore, how and why our teachers and kids' workloads are so much higher than those of regular-orthography nations. We'd also consider how much higher still they'd be, if our kids and Estonian kids had to learn equivalent content in that third year of schooling.

We'd also consider and explore how regular-orthography schools are time-rich and text-rich, while we're both time-poor and text-poor.

Their History, Science and Geography texts can use any wording they choose, while ours must have easy words and wording, to support our kids' weak word-reading.

Bunyips in the Classroom: The 10 Changes

For writing, regular-orthography Grade 2 kids transfer their thoughts into writing easily, effortlessly and quickly; while our Year 2 kids write slowly and laboriously, pausing lots to think about how to spell difficult words, and often sacrificing vocabulary, by avoiding words they consider hard to spell.

Yes, regular-orthography schools have ample time, and this enables them to achieve rich, exciting learning, because their Grade 2 kids are so highly literate and so much more effective learners, while we lag behind, time-pressured and scaffolding our kids' much weaker learning, as best we can.

It's two paradigmatically different education worlds, isn't it: regular-orthography nations' world of Es, and Ease, of Easy, Expedited, Efficient, Effective Education vs our sad world of Cs and Complexity?

It's time to say *Enough!* to us being that Chaotic, Cluttered-Curriculum Nation with Confused, Complex Learning, and excessive Cognitive load, ever wrestling with our Confused, Chaotic, Complicated, Cluttered-Curriculum Conundrum of too much to teach in too little time.

I'm fairly confident that if we asked our teachers which world they'd prefer to teach in, they wouldn't choose here now. Another bunyip.

Sadly, we've not just the factory's Nasty Byproducts 1, 2 and 3: too slow early-literacy development, too many weak learners with major struggles, and inefficient subject-area learning. We've also Nasty Byproducts 4 to 8:

- Nasty Byproduct 4: our Find the Learning Time Challenge.
- Nasty Byproduct 5: our Find the Caring Time Challenge.
- Nasty Byproduct 6: our too high child workload.
- Nasty Byproduct 7: our too high teacher workload.

Together, these four give us Nasty Byproduct 8: ineffective education generally.

These nasty byproducts are due to our kids' instructional needs, that in turn increase teacher workload.

They set off a chain of events that results in inadequate education for all kids, struggling and thriving alike.

In consequence, the factory then produces
- Nasty Byproduct 9: discouraged kids and unruly classrooms.
- Nasty Byproduct 10: the enormous difficulty we have in improving education.

In improving education, regular-orthography nations are highly manoeuvrable racing yachts that change direction quickly and efficiently. They action effective improvement initiatives quite easily – because kids are highly-literate, confident learners, and schooling is generally going well.

In contrast, we're more the Titanic: we've panicked, anxious awareness of desperate needs for huge, positive change, but we move far too slowly, despite our enormous efforts, with our turning towards improvement being agonisingly slow.

We're awash with lack-of-improvement inertia, being too loaded up with immature literacy and learning skills, struggling readers, unruly classrooms, and time-pressure, with too much to teach and learn in too little time.

Bunyips, anyone?

Yes, the impacts of our Early Years Factory and its nasty byproducts perpetuate Australia's education struggles.

It's now time to stop treading water, and make needed 10 Changes improvements.

Change 10 is *Build needed research knowledge as quickly as possible: Use collaborative school-based research.* Let's build the knowledge we need towards 10 Changes improvements quickly, efficiently and effectively.

Then let's action the key changes that our research shows are needed.

Our Disappointing Reading Results

> *By Year 3, there are wide differences in children's level of achievement in learning areas such as reading and mathematics. Some children are already well behind year-level expectations and many of these children remain behind throughout their schooling.*
>
> *Many are locked in the trajectories of 'underperformance' that often lead to disengagement, poor attendance and early exit from school.*
>
> Geoff Masters[xvii], 2016

The challenge of ongoing excessive numbers of struggling readers with major literacy and learning difficulties is our nemesis. It must be overcome if we're to improve education here, for all our kids.

Let's take a moment to consider reading and our reading results, showing where we are now, which is, of course, where we'd rather not be.

Capital-R Reading and small-r reading

Successful reading is having strong reading-comprehension skills that one uses effectively when reading texts, to obtain meaning and to reflect on it.

I'm terming reading comprehension, *Capital-R Reading*. That's because understanding what we read is our key reading skill, and why we so love our favourite books.

I'm terming word-reading, *small-r reading*. It's the reading of words in texts, and isolated words and word-parts. It's a subskill of reading comprehension – we have to read the words to access the meaning of what we're reading.

Experienced readers seldom notice their word-reading. It's automatic, and their focus is overwhelmingly on taking in the meaning of what is being read.

Until kids are quite skilled and confident readers, however, small-r reading is a major aspect of reading. It consumes kids' time, thinking and working memory, and heightens cognitive load, and also reduces their working memory for comprehension. More bunyips.

Because Standard English word-reading is so difficult and slow to develop, word-reading is a vastly bigger issue for the Anglosphere than it is for regular-orthography nations. That's another bunyip.

A further bunyip is the minimal university training needed by pre-service teachers in regular-orthography nations, to be expert at word-reading and spelling instruction for all kids, including slower-developing learners. One professor told me universities need allocate just one week to study both teaching and remediation. Clearly that works well, given they've such strong word-reading and spelling.

They succeed with minimal training, while we need years of training but still have far too many struggling readers.

Yes, English orthographic complexity means both Capital-R and small-r reading are extremely important here.

Struggling Readers Are Struggling Communicators

In understanding our struggling readers' needs, we need to consider not just cute koala kids' reading comprehension and word-reading skills, but also their language skills.

We all use many and varied language skills, every moment of every day, and kids' effective development of language skills plays a very major role in life, learning, and academic and life achievements.

Language skills are central to all communication. They're thus central to Capital-R Reading and all learning.

Language skills that kids need for effective communication, literacy and learning include
- Receptive and expressive vocabulary.
- Language comprehension (understanding).
- Language expression in speaking and writing.
- Language reasoning and thinking skills such as logical and social reasoning, subtlety and inferencing.
- Effective use of these skills in the many contexts where listening, speaking, reading and writing are used.

Language skills also include key cognitive-processing skills developed from early childhood – skills that are vital for communication and complex learning. They include
- Phonological and phonemic awareness.
- Phonological-verbal (auditory) short-term and working memory.
- Retrieval skills, including processing speed and Rapid Automised Naming (RAN).
- Executive-function skills.

Not surprisingly, studies are showing that weak language skills are a massive issue dragging down our kids' literacy skills, their academic achievement and education generally. Australian reports, from the Murdoch Children's Research Institute, the Deeble Institute, and Speech Pathology Australia, detail the situation:
- Large numbers of kids, quite likely at least 20%, have major language-skills weakness.
- Lack of free, easily-accessed services is a huge barrier preventing kids from receiving intervention.
- Ignoring language weakness has insidious impacts, including major reading, literacy and learning difficulties, behaviour difficulties, and severely reduced employment and adult-life opportunities.

We've bunyips in the classroom, once more.

Kids' language difficulties are a serious public-health issue in Australia, e.g., studies show that many of our Australian teenagers who run foul of our justice system have significant language weakness.

Our language-weakness epidemic is a very major issue, impacting kids, families, schools and education in major ways. It's imperative we resolve that epidemic, as part of leaving our struggling-education woes behind.

Much Vs Minimal: Our Reading Comprehension and Word-Reading Data

It's easy to consider reading-comprehension achievement, our kids' Capital-R Reading levels, as we've extensive reading-comprehension data to consider, from our NAPLAN testing of our Year 3, 5, 7 and 9 kids each year, and from PIRLS and PISA studies.

That data allows us to consider our cute koalas' reading-comprehension skills, for all three thirds of kids, at school, state, national and international levels.

In strong contrast, we've dismally limited understanding of our kids' skills on word-reading and language skills – reading-comprehension's two major subskills. That's due to further bunyips – our having virtually no data on those skills – because we don't test and monitor them.

Studies explored in *The Research Tours* show language weakness is prevalent in both our pre-schoolers and school kids. They also show that language weakness often goes unnoticed. Lack of data on kids' language skills is likely a major factor in our language epidemic. It results in kids with language weakness all too often not being identified.

Other nations test and teach vocabulary as a major education strand, but not us. We need to change so we've comprehensive knowledge of our kids' levels of different language skills, and provide strategic, tailored instruction.

In doing so, let's not just focus on receptive vocabulary as other nations do. Let's also focus on other important language-skill areas, including expressive vocabulary and word-finding, grammar, inferencing and logical reasoning.

We'd learn lots if, as part of online NAPLAN testing, we assessed 10% of our Year 3, 5, 7 and 9 kids across states and territories on this range of language skills.

Fortunately, for our healthy-progress word-readers, their reading-comprehension results give a good indication of their language-skill levels. That's not the case for weak word-readers, as poor word-reading drags down reading comprehension results. Our older cute koalas with healthy language-skill levels can have low reading-comprehension ages of 6.5 to 7.5 years purely because they've weak word-reading skills. We thus can't rely on reading-comprehension data to give us a full picture for our lower achievers.

Unfortunately, word-reading and language-skills weakness all too often flies under the radar here – because NAPLAN, PIRLS and PISA don't test those skills, and relatively few schools assess them across the years.

In addition, word-reading and its testing are an extremely divisive *Reading Wars* issue in education across the decades, here and in other Anglophone nations. Because of this, we've minimal current and historical data on our kids' word-reading levels.

That's appallingly inefficient, given we need to and want to improve education here in major ways.

In upper-primary and high-school kids I've assessed, I find major word-reading difficulties are prevalent, usually along with language weakness. With their schools not testing word-reading beyond the early years, or language skills, these kids have had considerable reading-comprehension intervention, but have missed out on the word-reading and language-skills intervention that they've needed.

Our schools really do need word-reading and language-skills data to use with their reading-comprehension data, if they're to tailor instruction effectively to kids' needs.

For now though, we've only reading-comprehension data to consider. So let's now consider that data, using our PISA and PIRLS reading-comprehension results. They provide quite provocative findings that are well worth considering.

Our PISA Tale of Decline

PISA, the Program for International Student Assessment, conducted by the OECD, tests 15-year-olds of many nations on Reading (reading comprehension), Maths and Science every three years. PISA began in 2000, with PISA 2018 the most recent round we have data on, at the time I'm writing.

Our PISA achievement pattern across those 18 years epitomises our education woes. It's bunyip time again.

Our PISA mean scores have steadily declined in all three subject areas, with numbers of low achievers steadily increasing, as numbers of high achievers steadily decrease.

We've room for improvement, that's for sure.

Using mean scores, in PISA 2018,
- Top achievers were regular-orthography and multilingual nations: China, Singapore, Hong Kong, Estonia, Canada, Finland, Ireland, Korea and Poland.
- Australia ranked 16th for Reading on average, with 10 nations significantly higher, 9 not significantly different, and 58 significantly below.
- USA, UK and NZ achieved just above us, but weren't significantly different.

Most high-achieving nations use regular orthographies or have high multilingualism. Multilingualism advantages learning, in ways similar to regular orthographies. Both of them heighten cognitive-processing, executive-functioning and learning skills.

Indeed, we'd benefit from studying the extent to which multilingualism and teaching practices relate to Canada and Ireland's significantly higher PISA achievement. After all, their kids are reading Standard English just as ours are, but they achieve significantly higher.

We'd likely also include our close neighbour, New Zealand, in those studies. It's interesting how, despite quite strong multilingual emphases in education, New Zealand doesn't seem to experience multilingual advantage in educational outcomes to the level that Canada and Ireland achieve.

It's possible that heightened impeding of word-reading and spelling might be happening for New Zealand, as Māori and Standard English vowel GPCs overlap in interesting ways. This might cause considerable confusion, and greater needs for strategic, systematic word-reading instruction for cute Kiwi beginning readers.

Our PISA Bell Clangers

Did you know that in PISA 2000, the first PISA round, Australia came sixth! We were immensely proud.

Alas, the bells were tolling even then that our too many struggling readers would be our undoing.

Bell clanger one: For our indigenous kids, our average score placed us second last of all nations for Reading – a grief-worthy bunyip. That's incredibly low, well worthy of both national and international shame.

Sadly, given our WYSYAINing talents, most of us didn't bat an eyelid, and simply accepted it as our status quo.

It's actually a HUGE issue. When a nation provides vastly less effective education for its indigenous kids, clearly it's in serious trouble and not meeting its teaching challenges in very major ways.

We need education that amply meets our indigenous kids' literacy and academic needs, whilst equally respecting, encouraging and emphasising important cultural themes.

Not surprisingly, given our extremely severe orthographic disadvantage, there's been no improvement in the outcomes of our indigenous kids in PISA. That's a sad bunyip.

We're in serious trouble, and it's time to recognise it.

Bell clanger two: We showed the widest gap of all nations between the Reading scores of our kids who chose to read outside of school for at least an hour a day, and the scores of our kids who didn't.

Of the PISA 2000 reluctant readers (kids not reading for pleasure out of school), ours showed seriously low reading comprehension, whereas the regular-orthography reluctant readers were strong readers who did well in PISA. That's an important bunyip, one future research should explore.

We largely treat our kids' lack of home reading as an issue of motivation, but this PISA finding suggests many don't read because their reading is excessively weak.

Australia showing the largest gap out of all the PISA nations suggests quite strongly that many in our long sad tail of underachievers lack the reading skills they need to be confident readers at home.

It also logically spotlights another important bunyip: in addition to their low reading-comprehension skills, many of our weak readers will have weak reading-comprehension subskills – weak word-reading skills, weak language skills, or weakness in both areas.

Australia really should assess the word-reading and language skills of all Aussie kids who participate in future PIRLS and PISA rounds. Having data on language skills, word-reading and reading-comprehension for PIRLS and PISA participants, plus data from 10% NAPLAN samples, would shed useful light on our kids' literacy strengths and weaknesses, and our education challenges.

PISA 2000 began the international race to educational improvement. It was the first time many nations saw how well they were doing relative to other nations, and it sparked interest in improving education internationally. Not surprisingly, as regular-orthography nations actioned their improvement agendas in deft racing-yacht style, they soared past us en masse.

With our too many struggling readers and time-pressured schools, we've continued Titanic style, working frantically but all too slow to turn from our lows towards improvement.

We still scored well in PISA 2003, but from PISA 2006 our woes became increasingly obvious.

Importantly, we didn't just drop down the rankings as other nations improved. Our results also dropped relative to our 2000 and 2003 results, and our numbers of high achievers dropped as our numbers of low achievers rose. Those bunyips alas smack of overwhelmed learners, far too busy teachers, and the widespread ineffectiveness of education here for all our cute koala kids.

Our performance in PISA 2018 is a sad montage of our high-school literacy and learning woes, and struggling education generally. We showed no improvement in Reading, Maths or Science, with an increased number of low achievers, and fewer high achievers.

For Reading, we had 40% of kids achieving below average level (Level 3) in 2000, which is bad enough, but this rose to 52% achieving below average in 2018. It's very sad, when over half our kids aren't managing to achieve at average level or above. For high achievers (above Level 4), in PISA 2000, we had 17%, our highest number. That has steadily dropped across PISA rounds: we'd just 13% in 2018.

It's important to note that we do have almost half our kids showing healthy reading in PISA, so it's not all bad. It's more that, if we want to think of Australia as a high-achieving nation with effective education, it's simply not good enough.

Having so many kids achieving below average level in PISA speaks volumes. It's clear we're not meeting our teaching challenges for at-risk and weak readers in major ways. These kids epitomise our needs for massive improvement.

PIRLS: A Tale of Sighs and Smiles

PIRLS is the *Progress in International Reading Literacy Study* that tests reading comprehension of 10-year-olds in many nations every five years. PIRLS 2001 was the first round, with subsequent rounds in 2006, 2011 and 2016. PIRLS 2021 data isn't available at the time I'm writing, so we'll just consider data from PIRLS 2001 to 2016.

On the whole, Australia's PIRLS and PISA performance and trends have been rather similar, with achievement dropping over time, and Australia always having excessive numbers of low achievers.

Fortunately, a refreshing change, PIRLS 2016 included very good news. We improved on average from 2011 to 2016, due to definite improvement in our middle and upper-third. Teachers and kids, take a bow – you work so very hard, and it's great to see this improvement. Here's hoping it flows on to stronger high-school achievement and improved PISA results in the future.

Alas, yet again, we showed no improvement in our low achievers, our crushed and crumpled koalas in their sad slog of struggles. We also showed yet again that we're failing to meet our teaching challenges for our indigenous kids and kids with low Socio-Economic Status (SES).

The lack of improvement in our low achievers is not at all surprising – with our teachers and schools so inadequately resourced, it's too big an ask for them to also catch-up our seriously-struggling learners.

Unruly Classrooms: Cause or Effect?

Using PISA 2018 data, an OECD report entitled *What school life means for students' lives* explored the extent to which 15-year-olds find their learning journey satisfactory.

Sadly, but not surprisingly from orthographic-disadvantage perspectives, we ranked poorly. Our schools' disciplinary climate ranked eighth worst in the world, with Australia scoring 69th out of 76 nations.

In addition to our academic struggles, our classrooms are amongst the unruliest in the world, in what's likely a nasty chicken and egg cycle. That's a grief-worthy bunyip, worthy of national shame. Did you realise how bad things are?

This is very real. Recently, a pregnant teacher friend shared how traumatised she had felt that day at school, trying to protect her bub while being the tough teacher on playground duty working to end a fight between two hefty Year 11 boys. She'd kept the tough exterior on till the kids were delivered to the office, then found a quiet spot on her own, where she burst into tears.

Behaviour issues are time-consuming. All too often, teaching and learning time is reduced, as is teaching effectiveness, because teachers must deal with behaviour issues. The OECD report only discussed high schools, but our problems are systemwide, impacting all school years. Violence against teachers is also increasing.

This is sad, horrific really, and most certainly unacceptable.

Our disciplinary climate ranking eighth worst in the world also speaks oceans about many kids' low levels of motivation and engagement in our classes, and the difficulties teachers have achieving effective teaching that meets each child's needs. More bunyips.

We don't want our kids in the world's most disruptive classrooms. We don't want our teachers there either. It's definitely time for highly effective change.

Interestingly, but not surprisingly, high-achieving regular-orthography and multilingual nations showed excellent disciplinary climates. That's logical given they're Easy Education Nations, vastly different to us, with virtually all kids being successful learners, learning difficulties being few and quite minor, and schools having ample teaching time.

Do you, like me, think that key factors contributing to our unruly classrooms include having too many kids with major reading and learning difficulties, and our teachers having far too high workload?

Do you, like me, think that the frustration kids experience because they're not sufficiently supported is also a factor?

Do you, like me, think that our teachers being too busy to adequately support kids is a factor, as is the frustration that teachers experience when, having worked their hearts out to progress struggling readers, so many make limited progress?

Do you, like me, think these are all factors in why so many of our wonderful teachers are leaving the profession?

Do you, like me, think that a lot of teachers would like to scream and yell just like the kids do, but instead restrain themselves then go to see a counsellor, blaming themselves for a perceived lack of needed skills? That's sad too, as the problem is not their skill levels, but systemic difficulties due to our struggling-education woes. More bunyips.

It's also a strong contrast of GENTLE and HEARTSH. Regular-orthography nations can easily achieve what I term GENTLE: *Gentle, Engaging, Never-Tiring, Learning Enrichment.*

That's almost impossible for Aussie schools to achieve on a routine basis because we're so time-pressured. All too often, we instead end up at HEARTSH: *Hugely-Exhausting, Actually-Rather-Tedious Schooling Heaviness.* School's not fun, and our kids and teachers are dispirited.

Certainly, research studies discussed in *The Research Tours* show behaviour difficulties to be a major school issue here. In addition, sadly, cute koalas with severe communication difficulties are more likely to be picked up for behaviour difficulties than communication weakness. More bunyips.

It does seem likely that underachievement, disengagement, frustration, too low resourcing and unruly classrooms are interrelated factors whose combined effects exacerbate our education challenges, including failure to reduce numbers of seriously struggling readers and overcome their difficulties, i.e., to meet our teaching challenges.

Further, with regular-orthography nations' education being GENTLE and our education HEARTSH, amidst bunyips many, it's really not at all surprising that we achieved eighth worst in the world for unruly classrooms.

Yes, Australian education is definitely struggling – and, if we're to end our education woes, our improvement needs to be at racing-yacht speed.

Let's Solve This!

Although the traditional focus has been on ensuring that all children are ready for school, equally important is ensuring that schools are ready and able to respond to the very different stages that children have reached upon entry to school.

Geoff Masters[xviii], 2016

It takes a village to raise a child – education is holistic, and schools can't do it all.

We need to treat our teachers professionally and ensure workloads are appropriate and very manageable, as so many other nations do.

We also need to ensure very manageable workload for all our cute koala kids.

We need to improve teaching and learning, plus the allied-health intervention services our at-risk kids receive, both before starting school, and across the school years.

We need to effectively meet our teaching challenges, to catch our vulnerable at-risk cute koala joeys before they fall, and put in the effort needed to ensure they achieve well, and enjoy ongoing success.

We need to achieve highly-effective, tailored education that meets each child's specific needs, not just for at-risk and struggling readers, but for all Aussie kids, upper, middle and lower-thirds alike.

Let's Solve This!

Nothing is surer than that, at the current time, Australian education needs massive improvement.

Equally, nothing is surer than that this is improvement that we most certainly can achieve.

We've marvellous potential for exponential improvement, by strategically actioning the 10 Changes.

The future is bright. Let's move there.

And let's start now.

PART 2
THE 10 CHANGES

Setting Our Goals

Before we explore each change, let's review the list of all 10 Changes, while thinking on how we'll best achieve them:

Change 1. Understand how orthographies matter: English spelling is dragging us down.

Change 2. Own our struggling reader woes: End hypocrisy and pretence.

Change 3. Weigh workload: Our children and teachers are working far too hard.

Change 4. One-size education does not fit all: Teach to the decidedly different instructional needs of upper-third and lower-third readers.

Change 5. End our data deficiency: Build strong knowledge on word-reading levels.

Change 6. Enrich every child: Ensure effective, supportive, tailored education.

Change 7. Insist on easier early-literacy development: Reach regular-orthography nations' achievement levels.

Change 8. Investigate the potential of fully-regular beginners' orthographies: Research shows they're key.

Change 9. First, play to learn: Start Standard English word-reading instruction from mid-Year 2.

Change 10. Build needed research knowledge as quickly as possible: Use collaborative school-based research.

Let's keep in mind our mantra, with many thanks to Jackie French[xix]:

There are no such things as reading difficulties.
There are only teaching challenges.

Let's also keep in mind our ABCs of improving of education, which we'll use as we enact 10 Changes improvements:

A. ACT locally while looking globally.

B. BOOST the lower-third to benefit everyone.

C. CHANGE effectively to work less and achieve more.

We can definitely turn around our complex struggling-education problem, and do this very successfully. Strong positive changes are achievable, at relatively low expense, if we explore methods other nations use with strong success.

By changing sensibly, using 10 Changes directions, we can progress delightfully, and if we choose to, excel.

Having goals that aren't specific so often leads to major inefficiency. I'm therefore providing a highly-specified goal:

> *By 2035, Australian education will be*
> *routinely, efficiently, gently and easily*
> *achieving highly effective, rapid development of*
> *children's word-reading, spelling, reading, writing*
> *and early-literacy skills,*
> *in GENTLE manner,*
> *in every early-years classroom,*
> *in all schools across our nation,*
> *as efficiently as is achieved routinely*
> *across schools in regular-orthography nations*
> *such as Taiwan, Japan and China,*
> *with at least 98% of Australian school children*
> *being confident, independent readers and writers,*
> *able to read 95% of the 10,000 most-frequent words,*
> *by age 8.5 years, or within 18 months of starting*
> *formal word-reading instruction.*

Now that's a useful, manageable goal. It's challenging but definitely achievable, and in precisely stating what we're aiming for, it encourages strategic consideration of the directions we need to take.

It could have been more challenging, requiring literacy development as rapid as nations with sole orthographies and highest orthographic advantage, e.g., Finland and Estonia.

I've instead set the bar lower, at literacy development as easy and rapid as that of Taiwan, Japan and China, where kids first master a fully-regular beginners' orthography, then subsequently master their complex orthography.

The goal is equitable and ethical, respecting our children's rights and entitlements to education that's no harder than is needed, and no harder than many leading nations achieve.

It prioritises keeping Standard English.

Logically, it intimates that we will investigate using a fully-regular beginners' orthography prior to Standard English, towards achieving faster, easier early-literacy development.

It also enables age-appropriate learning and investing our first 2.5 years of schooling in enriching kids' language and thinking skills. We'd then commence formal literacy and numeracy learning from mid-Year 2, when we'd be teaching to confident, literate kids with mature learning skills, who are far more ready for the challenges of Standard English.

In Part 2, we're now going to explore each of the 10 Changes, in turn. Each will play a strong role in our transforming of education.

Australian education needs to consider them, then explore them, as separate and integrated changes, building the knowledge needed to take action in logical directions.

The research needed to establish their value could be achieved within a few years, and shouldn't be allowed to take too long.

Change 1
Understand How
Orthographies Matter

Knowingly or unknowingly, countries have adopted orthographies that favour either the early stages of learning to read or the advanced stages, that is, the experienced reader.
The more a system tends towards a one-to-one relationship between graphemes and phonemes, the more it assists the new reader and the non-speaker of the language, while the more it marks etymology and morphology, the more it favours the experienced reader.

Richard Venezky[xx], 2004

Change 1 states, *Understand how orthographies matter: English spelling is dragging us down.*

We simply must give English orthographic complexity vastly more respect than we've given it to date. Let's have more and more of us well aware of the massive differences that orthographies make in education.

We've been overlooking and ignoring Standard English's many and varied negative impacts far too long.

We've thus bunyips galore. Our failure to effectively manage orthographic complexity across our kids' early-literacy development, from start of school, causes major stress and struggles for our cute koalas, teachers, schools and nation.

Importantly, we must stop thinking that complex spelling only impacts learning to spell. Its strongest impact is on word-reading, and weak word-reading impedes literacy and learning far more than weak spelling blocks writing.

Yes, our spelling difficulties are indeed a big issue, but they take a back seat to our word-reading issues, including the word-reading difficulties too many cute koala kids have, which underlie their literacy and learning struggles.

Exploring Regular Orthographies

Orthographies differ in many ways, e.g., they range from highly-regular through to highly-complex, and nations differ in how many orthographies they use.

There's enormous value in us exploring the differences in literacy development between nations that use different orthography options. Let's include

- Standard English readers in predominantly monolingual nations, e.g., the UK and Australia.
- Standard English readers in high-achieving multilingual nations, Canada and Ireland.
- Kids in Easy Education Nations with single highest-regularity orthographies, e.g., Finland, Estonia and South Korea.
- Kids in role-model Semi-Easy Education Nations, Taiwan, Japan and China, who read and write a fully-regular beginners' orthography initially, before transitioning to their complex orthography.

As part of that, there'd be huge value in exploring the skill development of kids at different levels of achievement. Let's use thirds plus finer groupings, including tenths (deciles), plus the lowest and highest 5% and 2% of achievers.

If you've not had exposure to highly-regular orthographies, it can be difficult to grasp the ease and speed of early-literacy development in regular-orthography nations.

When first reading on this area in the early 2000s, our CQU research team considered the findings of research studies somewhat surreal, almost unbelievable in fact.

Bunyips were jumping everywhere. If the expedited early-literacy development of regular-orthography kids was truth, then, frankly, we Australians and the Anglosphere are guilty of decades of damaging WYSYAINing – all the decades since the Anglosphere's Initial Teaching Alphabet (ITA) research of the 1960s showed easy, rapid, early-literacy development and dramatically reduced numbers of struggling readers.

To understand what was really happening, we couldn't do it at a distance. We needed to visit schools and researchers in regular-orthography nations.

Thus, in 2005, our CQU team met with researchers and visited schools in USA, Finland, Estonia, Italy, Scotland, England and Wales.

We were soon firmly convinced of the ease and advantages of regular orthographies for beginning readers. We've since developed models and *Orthographic Advantage Theory* and written widely on this area.

Let me briefly show you a regular orthography. You'll soon see how easy it makes learning to read and spell.

Have a go at reading this text. And if it seems a tad tricky, do identify with how our struggling readers feel every day.

Wuns upon u tiem thair wer three litul pigz hooo livd in u kotuj with thair muthu.

Wun dae muthu pig sed tooo her kidz, 'It's tiem for yooo tooo bild yor oen howzuz.' Soe of thae went.

Thu ferst litul pig met u farmu with a loed of stror.

'Pleez cood I hav sum ov yor stror?' thu pig arskt pulietlee.

'Sertunlee, yooo fien yung pig,' ansud thu farmu, hooo gaev thu litul pig az much stror az woz wontud.

The orthography is my Stage-1 Fleksispel. Fleksispel can be either a single-stage fully-regular beginners' orthography, or a multi-stage orthography, with Stage 1 supporting regular-orthography learning and earliest-literacy development, and

Change 1 Understand How Orthographies Matter

then Stages 2 to 5 supporting kids' transitioning to Standard English, and our teaching and learning of Standard English.

Fleksispel is free for use by non-commercial educators and researchers keen to explore English regular-orthographies. A file on Fleksispel is available on ResearchGate.

Stage 1, below, is fully regular. Stages 2 to 5, the successive transitioning stages from fully-regular Stage 1 through to Standard English (Stage 6), each have a very manageable amount of content to be taught and learned.

Fleksispel - Stage 1
41 Grapheme-Phoneme Correspondences (GPCS)

19 Vowel GPCS		22 Consonant GPCS					
ae m*ae*t	**ar** m*ar*t	**b** bat	**n** nat	**sh** *sh*at
a mat	**er** m*er*t	**d** dat	**p** pat	**ch** *ch*at
ee m*ee*t	**or** m*or*t	**f** fat	**r** rat	**th** *th*at
e met	**ow** n*ow*	**g** gat	**s** sat	**ng** ta*ng*
ie m*ie*t	**oo** f*oo*t	**h** hat	**t** tat		
i mit	**ooo** m*ooo*	**j** jat	**v** vat		
oe m*oe*t	**oy** b*oy*	**k** kat	**w** wat		
o mot	**air** h*air*	**l** lat	**y** yat		
ue m*ue*t		**m** mat	**z** zat		
u mut					
u sistu (ə)					

All that's needed to read and write Stage-1 Fleksispel is to learn its letter-sounds: its 41 graphemes and the sound each one says, i.e., its GPCs. That might sound hard, but it's not – it's as easy as kids' learning their letter-sounds now.

Knowing Fleksispel's letter-sounds (GPCs), you'd learn to sound-out Fleksispel as you read and write. This takes very little time, e.g., how quickly can you read this sentence: *Mie nue boet iz u buetee*. You'd also write words, first slowly then with increasing speed. And that's it, learning completed.

Using Fleksispel Stage 1, once you know your letter-sounds (GPCs) and how to sound-out in reading and writing, you can read every word and write all words, slowly at first, then with increasing speed. Congratulations!

What's more, you won't need any outside help. With all words so easy to read and write, you'd very soon be a successful, independent, self-teaching reader and writer.

That learning is very manageable:
- Complexity and cognitive load – extremely low.
- Hours taken – very few.
- Support needed – minimal.
- Likelihood of learning difficulties – extremely low, because the learning is so delightfully simple.

That's the blissful ease of regular orthographies.

Looking at Fleksispel's spelling patterns (GPCs), you can see how very similar it is to Standard English. The Consonant GPCs are identical, and the vowel GPCs are logical Standard English spellings. All graphemes are common GPCs of Standard English, apart from *ooo* as in *moo* (*m*ooo). Every GPC is one-to-one, apart from *u* which is used for two sounds, its common vowel sound as in *mut*, and also the schwa – because many beginners write the schwa as *u* in early writing, e.g., *muthu, tigu, yestuday*.

In Fleksispel, each phoneme will be written with just its single grapheme and no others, with no confusion, rather than with Standard English's prolific, confusing GPCs.

It would be a case of Fleksispel's *f* vs Standard English's four graphemes *f, ff, ph, gh*; and Fleksispel's *or* vs Standard English's 14 and more graphemes, e.g., *or, ore, our, our_e, aw, awe, ough augh, au, au_e, al, oar, (w)ar, (s)ure*.

The difference really is just the consistency and calm of Fleksispel, which is utterly regular and trustworthy, and thus perfect for early-literacy learners. Its use would build strong skills and confidence, and hold back the confusion of Standard English until kids are ready for it, while building the cognitive-processing skills they need.

Change 1 Understand How Orthographies Matter

Like Fleksispel, the Initial Teaching Alphabet (ITA), which the Anglosphere used widely in the 1960s, was very similar to Standard English. For multi-letter graphemes, where I've used underlining, ITA used joined letters. Here's ITA, below.

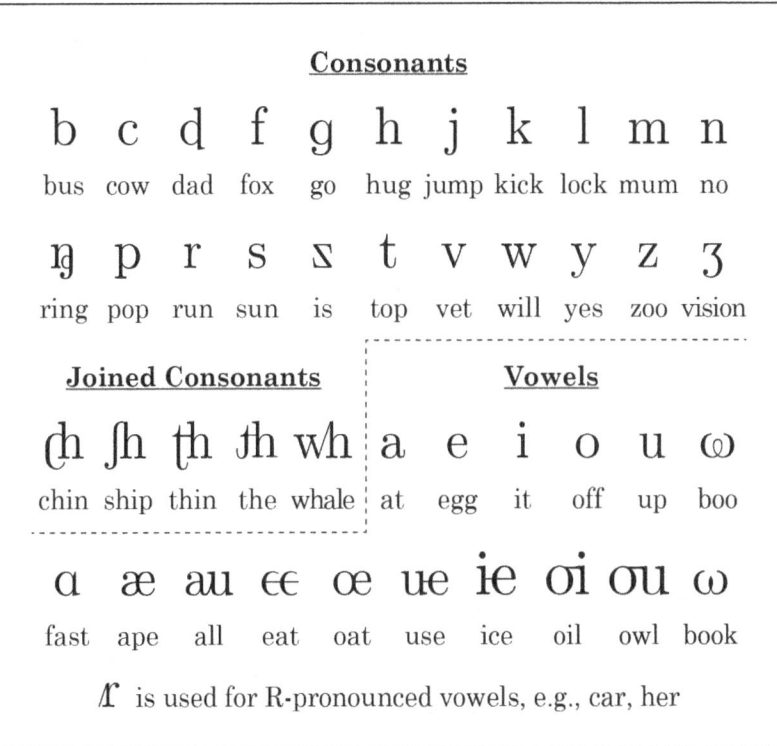

Both ITA and Fleksispel have similar and identical GPCs to Standard English. This expedites transitioning, making it easy for all three thirds of kids, especially if highly-irregular words in texts kids read are written in both the beginners' orthography and Standard English.

In transitioning from ITA, some words would be identical, while others would be highly similar. In transitioning from Fleksispel, all highly regular words and syllables will be identical, e.g., *cat, boy, car, crash, lunch, kidnap, padlocking*.

Kids would still have to learn to read and spell our many less-regular words, but they'd be nicely ready for it, and handle it vastly more easily than they do now, because of the strong phonological and orthographic-awareness, executive-function and self-teaching skills they'd have built through reading and writing the regular orthography.

Our kids' transitioning to Standard English will be vastly easier than Taiwanese, Japanese and Chinese children's transitioning, because Standard English and our beginners' orthography would be so similar in many ways.

In contrast, there's virtually no overlap between Taiwan, Japan and China's beginners' and complex orthographies. That means their kids have lots to learn, as they transition.

Their beginners' orthographies are very simple, as simple as Fleksispel Stage 1 and ITA, and thus mastered very easily.

In contrast, their complex orthographies are inordinately complex compared to Standard English, and involve vastly more learning.

In many ways, each of their thousands of individual characters kids learn, are akin to our most irregular sightwords, e.g., *who, echo, sugar, antique, tough, though*, which involve considerable visual memorising.

Nonetheless, because their kids have heightened literacy and learning skills, they nonetheless cope well with all that highly-complex learning, and transition impressively well.

This can be seen in the strong results these nations achieve by middle primary school, in PIRLS reading studies.

Because our beginners' orthography would be so similar to Standard English, our children would transition far more quickly and efficiently. Indeed, many children would take very little time for most word-reading: they'd soon be reading Standard English confidently and well, slowly at first then with increasing speed and fluency.

Mastering spelling of our haphazard schwa spellings, single vs double consonants, and infrequent more-irregular words would take time, but this wouldn't overly interfere with kids' writing fluency, if we allowed and encouraged use of regular-orthography spellings in first draft writing.

Regular-orthographies make schooling easy. They ease and speed both early literacy and subject-area learning.

They keep cognitive load and teacher and child workload low, and save hugely on teaching and learning hours – the hours we currently spend building reading and writing of Standard English.

In doing so, they create an Easy Education world that is paradigmatically different from our current Aussie world of reading and education woes.

We really should join that Easy Education world.

We Do It for Handwriting

We do it for handwriting now – initially keeping learning as simple as possible, then moving to more complex learning later, after kids are adept with the early, simpler skills.

Let's now also do it for reading and writing, keeping learning as simple as possible by our use of a fully-regular beginners' orthography, before transitioning kids to Standard English.

It really is the same principle.

We initially keep handwriting as simple as possible, with kids just using printing, often just using lowercase letters initially, then adding in capitals as kids' skills build.

Then, when kids are writing confidently and well, we transition them to writing cursive script (*running writing*).

In a similar manner, we'd use our fully-regular English beginners' orthography to keep word-reading and spelling delightfully simple until children are confidently reading and writing, then we'd transition them to reading and writing Standard English.

It's that simple. It may not seem that way to you at present, but that's just WYSYAIN.

As Nelson Mandela[xxi] so wisely said, *It always seems impossible until it's done.*

English Spelling: Where Confusion Meets High Cognitive Load

While we use solely Standard English without a beginners' orthography, our beginners soon frequently encounter about 200 spelling patterns:

- Our commonest letter-sound GPCs for letters and common digraphs *sh, ch, th, ng*.
- Our common two-letter vowel GPCs, e.g., *ai, ea, oa, ie*.
- Our R, Y and W vowel GPCs, e.g., *ar, er, ir, or, ur, ear, air, ear, y, ay, oy, aw, ew, ow*, which beginners, not surprisingly, initially try to read as separate sounds, e.g., as *a-r* as in c*ar*rot, not *ar* as in c*ar*.
- The contrasting GPCs in many highly-frequent words, e.g., b*a*ll/b*a*t, b*u*t/p*u*t, w*a*s/h*a*s, c*a*r/c*a*t, p*u*ll/d*u*ll, g*o*/t*o*, th*en*/th*ey*, wh*o*/h*ow*, w*or*k/w*al*k, h*e*/h*er*/h*ere*, wh*ere*/w*ere*/w*e're*, h*o*me/s*o*me, w*ou*ld/w*or*ld, it's/its, h*or*se/h*ou*se, n*igh*t/*eigh*t, c*oul*d/c*ol*d, *o*ne/d*o*ne/b*o*ne, t*o*/tw*o*/t*oo*, wr*i*te/r*igh*t, y*ou*/y*our*, th*eir*/th*ere*/th*ey're*, b*ear*/h*ear*/h*ear*d, b*oy*/b*ay*/b*y*, g*o*/g*oes*/g*o*ne, en*ough*/th*ough*/thr*ough*/thor*ough*, s*ay*/s*ays*/s*aid*, d*oes*/g*oes*.

This orthographic complexity creates major confusion and masses of drawn-out, complicated learning. In addition to large workload, it also creates ongoing, high cognitive load, not just when kids are learning to read and write, but also when they're reading and writing in subject-area learning.

This high workload doesn't happen in regular-orthography nations, not even Taiwan, Japan, and China. That's because, after using a fully-regular orthography, their kids' learning is very efficient, plus character learning is in neat year-level portions, and reading materials are well aligned.

English orthographic complexity, poorly managed, gives us appallingly slow early-literacy development and sadly high cognitive load. It also gives us our many struggling readers – approximately a third of our kids. Their major needs for remediation and learning support in turn add massively to teacher workload, with schools' meagre resourcing for learning support inevitably overwhelmed.

It's Bullet Trains Vs Railway Handcarts

The destination that all nations aim for in early-literacy development is confident, successful, independent literacy and academic learning.

Trains make a useful analogy for thinking on the speed and efficiency of that literacy and academic learning, and how quickly and effectively kids reach that success destination.

The Regular-Orthography Bullet Train

Healthy-progress regular-orthography word-readers and spellers ride the Bullet Train to success. It's unbelievably fast by our standards, and most kids can read and write words as accurately as adults do, before the end of Grade 1.

The Regular-Orthography Express Train

Slower-progress regular-orthography word-readers and spellers, perhaps their weakest tenth, travel on the Express Train to success. It's somewhat slower than the Bullet Train, but lightning fast compared to early-literacy here.

These kids reach the success destination usually by Grade 3 or 4, well ahead of most of our healthy-progress kids, because their accuracy difficulties for regular-orthography word-reading and spelling are so easily addressed.

Our Standard-English Slow Train

While some of our exceptionally fast developers will ride the Express Train, only our geniuses ride the Bullet Train. Most of our Standard English cute koala kids with healthy-progress word-reading and spelling, by our standards, will ride our Slow Train.

It's oh-so-slow, taking our kids at least six and nine years, on average, for kids to be reasonably proficient, but still far below regular-orthography kids' accuracy levels.

Our Standard-English Railway Handcarts

It's abysmally slow, exhausting Railway Handcarts that our poor, struggling, crushed and crumpled word-readers and spellers ride.

They've woefully insufficient skills for mastering reading and writing of Standard English, and are soon far behind the Slow Train, and a world away from the Express Trains and Bullet Trains of regular-orthography nations.

Life for them is lonely, isolating and exhausting, and the success destination all too often seems unreachable.

Even working furiously, they make only quite tiny gains, thus becoming further and further behind, with even the Slow Train long since disappeared over the horizon.

Oh for regular-orthography Bullet Trains and Express Trains! We want them and we need them.

And how sad it is for our cute koala kids and education here, with our kids riding Slow Trains and Railway Handcarts.

Which trains would kids in Taiwan, Japan and China ride?

While research is needed, we'll likely find they mostly ride Express Trains:
- Their kids develop impressive learning skills as they read and write their regular orthography.
- Words are written in both orthographies, side by side, in kids' reading books, and this expedites and maximises fluency, self-teaching and transitioning.
- Kids have nicely-achievable year-level sets of characters, which keep learning very manageable.

Given that our kids would transition in weeks and months, rather than Taiwan, Japan and China's years, which trains would our kids ride if we used a fully-regular beginners' orthography prior to Standard English?

There's every likelihood most cute koalas would ride Bullet Trains, not just Express Trains. We'd love that.

Orthographic Advantage and Disadvantage

Orthographies, the spelling systems nations choose to use, are incredibly important.

Highly-regular orthographies enable immense advantages for nations: they have strong orthographic advantage.

In contrast, highly complex orthographies used without a fully-regular beginners' orthography guarantee extreme disadvantage at child, schooling and national level.

In Australia, strong orthographic disadvantage reigns. It will continue to reign for as long as we start our wee koala joeys on solely Standard English in poorly resourced schools, thus ensuring continuance of our Early Years Factory and Spelling Generations.

Our CQU team developed *Orthographic Advantage Theory* as a useful tool for reflecting on crosslinguistic differences, and considering orthographic impacts on children, schools and nations, and how orthographic impacts contribute to our current education woes.

When a nation's children learn to read quickly and easily, with few experiencing difficulties, this offers proliferating advantages for individuals and the nation, including

- Ease of learning to read and write.
- Ease of teaching and learning across the school years.
- Ease of improving reading and education outcomes.
- Adults having the life advantages of high literacy.
- Generational advantage, through parents being proficiently literate and thus able to read to their children and support their literacy development.
- Workplace and economic advantage.

When a nation's children are slow to learn to read and write, with many experiencing severe ongoing literacy difficulties, this creates corresponding disadvantage.

The orthographies nations choose, and how they manage them, impact national functioning in countless ways. I'll list here a mere 16 of those impacts:

1. National word-reading, spelling and literacy levels.
2. The number of risk factors with potential to derail at-risk children.
3. The extent to which those risk-factors are activated.
4. Ease of mastering word-reading, spelling, reading, writing and self-teaching.
5. Ease of developing phonemic awareness (needed for

Standard English word-reading and spelling).
6. The extent of school and homework hours needed for learning to read and spell effectively and well.
7. Early-literacy child and teacher workload for literacy and subject-area teaching and learning.
8. The cognitive-load levels kids and teachers experience.
9. Ease of subject-area learning.
10. Numbers of children and adults with word-reading and writing difficulties.
11. The severity of their difficulties.
12. The extent of resourcing needed to remediate kids' literacy learning difficulties.
13. The extent of resourcing needed to achieve effective literacy in all children.
14. Socio-Economic Status (SES) impacts on likelihood and extent of learning difficulties.
15. Ease of improving education.
16. Workplace literacy levels.

Those 16 aspects reflect both the orthographic advantage that regular-orthography nations can enjoy, and conversely our severe orthographic disadvantage. They also highlight quite a few bunyips.

Orthographic impacts are massive, aren't they?

Change 1: Understand How Orthography Matters

Change 1 is pivotal if we're to improve education here: *Understand how orthographies matter: English spelling is dragging us down.*

Let's do that, build widespread understanding of just how much orthographies matter.

In doing so, we'll steadily make retirement plans for a host of cheering bunyips.

Let's work to have lots and lots of Aussies increasingly aware of, and interested in, how the orthographies we choose make immense differences, and how much English orthographic complexity relentlessly drags down not just our kids' literacy development, but also Australian education.

Change 1 Understand How Orthographies Matter

We currently live with severe orthographic disadvantage, because we don't manage English orthographic complexity efficiently and effectively for our beginning readers.

This keeps us on the back foot, in our Early Years Factory with its nasty byproducts, enduring major child, educational and national disadvantage.

Understanding how orthographies matter, and their very major impacts on education and life, is a step we must take if we're to expedite improvement in Australian education.

Change 2
Own Our Struggling Reader Woes

Virtually every Australian with a disability encounters human rights violations at some point in their lives and very many experience it every day of their lives.

National People with Disabilities & Carer Council[xxii], 2009

Australia's major weaknesses relative to high achieving nations include too many weak readers, failure to improve reading outcomes, and significantly poorer achievement by indigenous children and children from low socio-economic status (SES) backgrounds.

Bruce Knight & Susan Galletly[xxiii], 2017

Change 2 is emphatic: *Own our struggling reader woes: End hypocrisy and pretence.* Let's do that.

Our Education Act[xxiv] is also emphatic:
Australian schooling will place the highest priority on
> a) Identifying and addressing the needs of school students, including barriers to learning and wellbeing;
> b) Providing additional support to school students who require it.

The Act clearly states that we must provide a rich and well-supported education for all Australian children, including those with learning difficulties. So too does our 2019 Alice

Springs (Mparntwe) Education Declaration. Importantly, so do the UN *Convention on the Rights of the Child* and *Convention on the Rights of Persons with Disabilities* that we're signatory to.

We've thus promised each and every cute koala kid a strong and effective education. But at the classroom coalface, our education norm is our kids missing out.

As an example, we've currently a distinct element of hypocrisy about the adequacy of the education and allied-health supports we provide our at-risk and struggling learners, both before school and across the school years. We're pretending they're great when that's not the case.

There seems an aura of pretence that all our kids with difficulties are being provided an ample, rich education that meets all their needs. And they're not!

Despite our Act prioritising the identification of kids' needs and provision of appropriate supports, for far too many crushed and crumpled koalas, the supports received are sorely insufficient.

Children with major language weakness and those with major literacy difficulties fit government definitions of disability. Their needs for support, for weak language and word-reading skills, should be identified and addressed.

But all too often, this doesn't happen.

Government websites discuss in glowing terms the supports our Federal and State governments provide, but these supports are all too often strong in theory, but sadly weak in practice.

Too many Aussie kids aren't being provided with the supports they need, so that they can have the effective education they are entitled to.

Their struggles position our Act's promises as rhetoric far more than reality.

We need to change that.

Avoided Responsibilities

It seems in many ways an issue of avoided government responsibilities.

How aptly ironic it was that the word that was accidentally misspelled on 46 million or so Australian $50 notes in 2019 was *responsibilty* (sic). Errors as regards responsibilities most certainly contribute to our current education woes.

Our government agencies seem to actively avoid meeting their responsibilities to provide needed education supports that our struggling readers have rights to.

Lack of national consistency seems a strong contributing factor. We've major differences in State definitions, criteria for funded disability categories, funding mechanisms and intervention systems; and this seems to enable agencies to avoid meeting their education and support responsibilities.

Also contributing are the overlaps between responsibilities, including those of
- Our State and Federal Governments.
- Our State and independent education systems.
- Our National Disability Insurance Scheme (NDIS) and our Health and Education departments.

There also seems lots of passing the buck.

There are also curious distinctions about whether kids have *difficulties, disorders* or *disabilities*. This is inappropriate: the issue is the kids' serious struggles, and those distinctions smack of disrespect for, and trivialising of, their difficulties.

It's all too common for our kids with Language, Literacy and Learning Disorder (LLLD), whether they've Developmental Language Disorder, Dyslexia or learning difficulties, to not receive supports they need, and thus continue to struggle.

Medical and allied-health professionals who work in private practice so often see kids who've been nastily buffeted by our sadly-inadequate health and education supports. Too often, we see major difficulties that should have been resolved years earlier, but haven't been, because early-childhood and school support services have been so meagre.

Towards avoiding evaded responsibilities, and given our Education Act's wording, there are compelling arguments for our education system to fund all relevant supports for school-age children, both in-school and out-of-school, as other nations do.

Our Governments' 2016 Sad Report Card

The 2016 Australian Senate report, *Access to real learning: The impact of policy, funding and culture on students with disability*, was highly critical of our government agencies for not meeting their responsibilities.

It discussed serious funding insufficiencies for children with learning disabilities, with reading disability referred to as a hidden disability, not sufficiently recognised or catered for in funding models.

It emphasised that many Aussie kids with disabilities don't receive the services they need and should be receiving[xxv]:

> Access to education is a basic human right, but for many students with disability in Australia, it is a right which they are prevented from accessing.

Importantly, it also highlighted a major lack of government transparency regarding children's needs and collected data.

Bunyips, anyone?

The Inadequacies of Education System Supports

When Aussie kids meet government criteria for official disability categories, their schools receive extra funding for needed resourcing for their educational supports.

Using Queensland as an example, and including categories relevant to struggling readers, the education system includes funded disability categories of Speech Language Impairment, Autism Spectrum Disorder and Intellectual Impairment, and hearing and physical impairments, with specific criteria kids must meet to attain these disability labels, so their schools can receive allocated funding.

However, there haven't been funding categories for Learning Disability and Attention Deficit/Hyperactivity Disorder (AD/HD). Further, kids with multiple significant disabilities who don't quite meet the eligibility cut-off scores for any one specific disorder don't receive special consideration for the severity of their combined difficulties. They thus miss out on funded disability support.

The situation across other states and territories is similar.

Our extremely-tight criteria and cut-off scores contrast markedly with those of the USA, which does a far better job than we do of prioritising and meeting responsibilities for ensuring kids' rights for supports are met.

Our funding categories and criteria seem questionable in many ways:

- It seems inappropriate that so many families have to pay privately for allied-health intervention supporting their kids' school functioning and learning, because those services aren't available through school.
- It seems inappropriate that allied-health services, both government and private are so often all too meagre.
- Given our education systems use a disability-category system, to omit a Learning Disability category seems curious and perhaps strategic.
- State criteria for the Speech Language Impairment category are excessively severe by international standards, thus vastly fewer kids here receive this funded support than happens, e.g., in USA schools.
- For the Speech Language Impairment category, states include a *Cognitive Referencing* eligibility criterion, an antiquated practice long rejected internationally, whereby kids' IQ scores must show a specific pattern of highs and lows – and kids with severe language weakness, who don't show that required IQ pattern, miss out on funded support.
- Accommodation for children with multiple disabilities, who score just outside the cut-off criteria for each individual disability, is lacking, with these kids often declared ineligible for funded disability support.

Quite frankly, our State and Federal Governments have seemed focused more on avoiding paying disability funding, than on supporting our cute koala kids who have disabilities, and their schools that so need this support.

The reason disability applications are submitted is because schools desperately need the resourcing that disability funding will provide. When kids miss out, with applications rejected, the lack of needed disability funding adds directly to class teachers' workload, as it's the kids' class teachers who must then provide all needed supports.

This leads to very disappointing situations – not least, kids' needs being severely overlooked, and our too busy class teachers being made even busier.

And, across the area, a crowd of bunyips can be seen.

Newsflash! Disability Funding Changes!

An impressive item hit the news the week before this book headed off to publication.

Queensland announced new disability categories, which would be eligible for disability funding, to start in 2023.

Dyslexia, Attention Deficit/Hyperactivity Disorder (AD/HD) Tourette Syndrome, Foetal Alcohol Syndrome, and mental health conditions will then be included as funded disability categories.

That's great that they're now to be prioritised. It will be interesting to see the eligibility criteria used, and the extent to which these kids, their teachers and their schools will be supported.

Let's Review Education System Responsibilities

We increase our education woes greatly when we fail to adequately support our crushed and crumpled koalas with severe learning difficulties, and their teachers.

Duplication and overlaps of government health, education and NDIS services are too often present. These enable easy evading of responsibilities, and are grossly inefficient, as our kids too easily slip through the cracks.

It's also not uncommon for kids to be dismissed, despite major needs, when agencies confidently refer them to other agencies, which don't actually provide the supports needed.

Towards greater systemic efficiency and kids' rights being met, things would work far more efficiently if our education system was responsible not just for all school supports, but also for all needed out-of-school interventions that support our kids' achieving of an effective education.

Further, given kids' development across pre-school years so strongly influences their school progress, there also seem arguments for education departments taking responsibility for children from 12 months of age, as other nations do.

NDIS Woes Reflect Education System Inadequacies

Now that we have the National Disability Insurance Scheme (NDIS) in action, families of many Aussie kids seek NDIS support. Many do this because of inadequate Education and Health system supports. Having missed out on needed supports both prior to and at school, for their struggling readers and learners, they now seek NDIS support for the allied-health interventions they need.

Indeed, NDIS now seems plagued by our State and Federal Education Departments' inadequacies in meeting both their responsibilities and teaching challenges.

The needs of many school kids with Language, Literacy and Learning Disorder (LLLD), i.e., Language Disorder and Dyslexia, would likely best be met by the education system.

Unfortunately, Education Departments haven't until now included the *Learning Disability* funding category that's much needed, where most severely-struggling readers would be identified. Thus many struggling readers and their schools miss out on much needed resourcing and supports.

Many of these kids meet NDIS disability criteria, thus families put in applications. NDIS is then plagued with applications for these kids in need, who've alas missed out on receiving needed supports at school.

Further, the kids who do receive funded school supports also plague NDIS – because the funded support schools receive is so often insufficient, and fails to meet their needs. That's unlikely to change, unless the extent of disability funding provided to schools for these kids increases markedly.

Much would be resolved if Education Departments took responsibility for meeting all kids' needs relevant to their achieving of an effective education.

Some families win the NDIS lottery and achieve needed funding. For others, all too often, applications are rejected.

Sadly, parents often report applications are rejected due to kids not having an education-system disability label.

There's somewhat sad irony there, as it seems very much double or nothing: kids who have school funding often also get NDIS funding, while kids who don't receive school funding all too often also miss out on NDIS funding, despite their reports showing their disabilities are at a severe level.

NDIS applications are rejected for lots of crushed and crumpled koalas whose reports clearly show their major disabilities. When kids don't have official school disability status, pressured NDIS staff perhaps decide that their difficulties must actually be quite minor, or assume their needs will be met within the education system.

There's also the issue that, if kids' difficulties seem to be predominantly disabilities impacting literacy and learning, NDIS staff deem these as not being NDIS responsibilities, instead declaring them education-system concerns.

Children with significant disabilities being rejected for NDIS funding raises serious questions of ethics and responsibilities. We're signatory to the UN Convention on the Rights of the Child and Convention on the Rights of Persons with Disabilities, plus our Act and documents promise supports, yet many kids with disabilities, are being discriminated against, with their rights to supports denied.

That said, children having major needs that NDIS staff consider should be met by schools also raises important issues regarding Education Department responsibilities.

This seems the heart of the matter – the extent of our Federal and State education systems' inadequacies and responsibilities. After all, the support needs of these children are towards them having equal opportunity to achieve an effective education that appropriately supports learning and progress, and empowers them for careers and adult life.

In addition, Language, Literacy and Learning Disorders (LLLD), including Developmental Language Disorder and Dyslexia, are lifelong disabilities needing ongoing supports.

We've a major ethical issue when kids with these disorders clearly meet NDIS criteria, but have applications rejected.

While their NDIS rejection is decidedly inappropriate, there really are much wider issues that bear deep consideration:

- Why are our struggling learners needing to look for NDIS funding when our Education Act, declarations and documents imply that needed supports should be provided by the education system?
- Why is it so difficult for struggling readers with language weakness and learning disabilities to get Education Department funded supports?
- Given that our states use disability categories, why has a Learning Disability category been omitted?
- Why is the level of funding provided for individual children with disabilities so often found inadequate?
- Why are our government criteria for disability categories so narrow, relative to other nations?
- Why are NDIS staff being placed in the situation where they're in effect forced to discriminate against children with disabilities on the basis of them not having an official Education Department disability label, given these kids have genuine major disabilities?

A phone message an NDIS staff member left for me said a boy I was working with would get NDIS funding but only if he acquired an ASD diagnosis at Level 2 severity, i.e., a respected education disability label. Quite frankly, the child had enough severe disabilities already, having severe Developmental Language Disorder, severe Attention Deficit/Hyperactivity Disorder (AD/HD), Inattentive type, and extremely severe Learning Disability, along with traits of Autism Spectrum Disorder (ASD).

It was clear this NDIS staffer understood that the child desperately needed supports. There seemed an underlying message that despite his stated severe disabilities, more was needed to tick the box to approve NDIS funding. The child didn't have ASD at Level 2 severity, thus family had to struggle on, with neither NDIS nor funded school support.

It is seriously inappropriate to position Australia's children and NDIS staff this way. Children with severe disabilities should be provided with needed services, and NDIS staff should not be forced to prevaricate.

Let's instead have our education systems fully meeting their responsibilities, and ensuring our cute koalas receive an amply-rich education, along with all needed supports.

We Need the Buck to Stop Here

Towards our Federal and State Governments meeting their responsibilities for providing educational supports, we're in strong need of *Someone in Charge*, an agency where the buck stops. This agency would stay the distance as families, teachers and schools discuss the inadequacies of the education and supports their particular struggling learner is receiving, with a social worker appointed to advocate for the child's interests, and the child's needs then being addressed, with appropriate supports allocated.

While at present there are agencies that families may appeal to, it's clear the current system is not working adequately for far too many kids, families and schools.

At an NDIS seminar that I attended, when NDIS was being introduced, the spokesperson stated very clearly that

- NDIS recognises that many families haven't received adequate Health and Education Department services.

- NDIS would not be funding this shortfall.
- It is families' responsibility to resolve their issues of inadequate Health and Education services.

That's a harsh but sensible statement, as NDIS funding is finite and must be carefully apportioned.

It highlights an important issue, however, that it's far too difficult for most families to battle things out with relevant government departments. It really is incredibly difficult for families to win through, when government agencies appear not to prioritise our kids' rights and support entitlements.

We thus need an agency that both respects and ensures our children's rights for pre-school and school support services.

Perhaps taking the form of a *Children's Educational Rights and Supports Ombudsman*, this central agency might have responsibility for ensuring the rights of Australian kids with learning difficulties or disabilities, and be the *Buck Stops Here* agency Aussies can appeal to, when kids' rights for education supports aren't being adequately met.

We Need a My State, My Nation Website

In association with this central agency, there also seems need for a national *My State, My Nation* website, using the exemplary openness of our *My School* website, which State and Federal Governments so enthusiastically instigated.

Aussie schools and parents, our rights aren't being met. Too often, it's too difficult for us to get clear information on education matters. An exemplary *My State, My Nation* website would provide the information we vitally need.

The 2016 Senate report slammed our governments' lack of transparency, and an effective *My State, My Nation* website could nicely turn this around. It could provide information on the similarities and differences of services, resources and disability criteria used in different states and nations.

If we're to improve education, it's important we make our inequities clearly evident, and easy to be considered.

The website could also list our kids' rights for education and allied-health supports as per our Acts and agreements.

It would include our Alice Springs (Mparntwe) Education Declaration, with its promises, along with the specifics of how kids' rights to promised supports will be actioned.

In addition, it could include access to that Buck Stops Here agency, suggested above, that families, schools and allied-health professionals could appeal to, in cases where cute koalas' rights to appropriate services and supports aren't being adequately met.

An effective My State, My Nation website could make a very positive difference in our improving of education here.

Government Responsibilities for Our Woes

There are clear government contributions to Australia's strong orthographic disadvantage.

They start with government responsibility for the age our kids learn to read, and for us using solely Standard English orthography without a beginners' orthography.

They then continue through insufficient supports being provided for kids whose major struggles are due largely to those government responsibilities for orthographies and the young age our cute koala joeys learn to read and write.

We start reading education at close to the world's youngest age, and expect our wee koala joeys to learn to read and write one of the world's most complex orthographies.

Whilst largely issues of WYSYAIN, they're also issues of government responsibilities and choices that cause much of our kids' literacy struggles and our education woes.

In this context of government choices causing much of our education woes, it is hugely disappointing that government actions cause our children's needs to be overlooked.

That's a bunyip. It is also a huge negative investment that heightens our education woes. In addition to being grossly unfair, it smacks strongly of our kids' rights being denied.

Our *Effective Literacy for All Students* Response

The 2016 Senate report clearly flagged our systemic inadequacies for struggling learners. In response, our CQU research team wrote a 2017 research article, *Effective literacy instruction for all students: a time for change*, using that Senate report, along with our 2013 Education Act and Australian disability documents.

Our article discussed the extent to which Australia has far more struggling readers than regular-orthography nations. It also explores possible reasons why Australia, a generally kind, compassionate democratic nation, might insufficiently support children with reading and literacy difficulties, given that these kids fit current government definitions of students with disabilities.

Certainly, the enormous expense of supporting all our struggling readers to the extent our Acts and agreements prescribe seems a possible reason for insufficient supports being provided.

After all, using Standard English initially with very young children guarantees that education will be stupendously expensive if all our kids with learning difficulties were to be provided with all the supports they should receive.

The article also explored the ethical appropriateness of using a disability category system that's not required by our Education Act, then omitting a Learning Disability category from that system.

The USA also uses a disability category system but a far higher proportion of their kids receive funded support because they include Learning Disability and other additional disability categories, plus they use considerably more lenient criteria, e.g., for Developmental Language Disorder, and for kids with multiple disabilities.

With Queensland now announcing changes, it will be interesting to see how our states compare with USA in the future, not just for the disability categories our education systems use, but also for the extent and types of supports that are provided.

Here's a useful example of our current Australian-USA contrast. I worked for some time with two brothers with severe Language, Literacy and Learning Disorder (LLLD). When the family moved back to the USA, the contrast of supports was disconcertingly massive.

Here in Australia, the family worked very hard at home, as did class teachers, but no disability labels or funded supports were forthcoming. While their school did its best, the learning support received was sadly insufficient; and the family paid privately for many sessions with me.

In the USA, with both boys soon identified as having funded disabilities, and rights that must be met, a plethora of supports ensued, both in-school and out-of-school, a veritable surfeit of riches.

The comparison was sobering, highlighting the unethical nature of the meagre supports our kids and schools receive.

It has never seemed appropriate that our children should require official disability labels for schools to receive much needed funding. Our kids and schools should receive the supports and resourcing they need without requirements for official diagnoses and arduous disability applications.

Given that our Education Act does not require a disability category system, there are strong grounds for moving to a more equitable support system with funding based on school and student needs, and ending requirements for disability labelling. This more ethical system might allocate school funding for all kids that schools identify in mid-Term 1 each year, with them then receiving tailored learning-support and allied-health interventions.

Since the 2016 Senate report's strong indictments on our education-system inadequacies, changes have occurred in Australian funding arrangements, not least the *Nationally Consistent Collection of Data* (NCCD).

Unfortunately, while adding to class teachers' workload, and creating administrative burden for schools' learning-support teachers, NCCD certainly hasn't improved the situation sufficiently.

Families of children with communication and literacy learning difficulties and the allied-health professionals, GPs and paediatricians working with them are well aware that the educational-support needs of these kids are still far from being sufficiently met. More bunyips.

Change 2: Own Our Struggling Reader Woes

Change 2 is *Own our struggling reader woes: End hypocrisy and pretence*. Actioning Change 2 is an essential step towards improving education for struggling readers, and education generally.

Too many vulnerable kids aren't getting adequate supports at school, or adequate allied-health supports before and across the school years.

Let's end that. We can't progress effectively while we pretend we're providing ample, suitable supports and that all is well, when all is not well, seriously so.

We need to build thorough understanding of the serious difficulties too many of our koala kids experience; the major inappropriate gaps in the supports they're provided; and, in consequence, our major needs for improvement in this area.

Let's own our struggling reader woes, and end hypocrisy and pretence.

Change 3
Weigh Workload

Extra effort, in whatever form it takes (mental, physical, emotional), cannot be sustained without eventual damage and diminishing returns.
There has to be a very acute awareness [of] the level of exertion and the toll it's taking.

Bill Walsh[xxvi], 2009

Change 3 states, *Weigh workload: Our children and teachers are working far too hard.* It's much needed.

Are we working our kids and teachers too hard? I'm confident we are, though I'm largely using logic here. It's Swiss-cheese research time, with sadly minimal research.

It's definitely an area we need to investigate.

Let's weigh workload, measuring our kids' and teachers' workload, the levels of stress entailed, the efficiency and effectiveness of that workload, and the impacts of key factors on workload and stress.

We Work Much Longer Hours

One workload indicator is the hours our children and teachers spend in classroom teaching and learning.

The 2015 OECD *Education at a Glance* report showed that our kids attend school for far more hours each year than most nations, at least 300 hours more than many leading nations. Our Australian kids' 1010 hours is sobering when compared with, e.g., Estonia's 661 hours, Finland's 632 hours, and Japan's 762 hours.

Now on the one hand, those extra school hours give us more teaching and learning time. On the other hand, our kids are more likely to be tired and less engaged, and hence be less efficient learners. That seems particularly so for our 5-year-olds who lack the resilience and maturity of older, more effective learners.

Reducing our kids' school hours is not a sensible solution, not until we have education working far more efficiently and effectively here. However, particularly across the early years, we need to change to strategically using our school hours in developmentally appropriate ways.

The 2015 OECD report also showed our teachers doing far more class-teaching hours each year than teachers in many nations. That's not good. Our teachers' 879 class-teaching hours contrasts severely with, e.g., Estonia's 619 hours, Finland's 677 hours, and Japan's 736 hours. That's a depressing bunyip – it's waving a placard saying *IT'S NO WONDER THAT EDUCATION IS STRUGGLING HERE!*

Now some might feel that the additional 200 hours means there should be ample time for mentoring children and providing individual support.

Alas, that's far from the case, as every teaching hour involves preparation, administrative duties and also often assessment. In addition, that extent of extra hours means teachers will often be teaching extra subjects and classes, and this entails further additional work.

It's appalling really. That 200 extra teaching hours shouts very loudly that we've major needs to reduce teacher workload, particularly given that we supply our class teachers with such low resourcing for their support of developing and struggling readers.

We treat our teachers as workhorses, not professionals, to a level that seems disrespectful. We demand they teach our children effectively in a professional manner, but then refuse them the supports and off-class time they need.

Education will not improve here without our teachers having appropriate off-class time. It's not needed just for teacher sanity and stress levels. Off-class time empowers teaching and kids' learning, being time for professional development, preparation, meetings, one-on-one work with children, mentoring, administration, marking, and much more.

It's curious how we treat allied-health staff professionally, but not our teachers, e.g., government-employed allied-health staff have far more off-client administration time. It's an extremely poor investment in our children's education when we provide others with useful administration time, but withhold it from our teachers. It's no surprise that teaching is becoming a less-preferred profession.

Our Struggling Readers Work Too Hard

Let's weigh the workload of all our three thirds of our kids. Let's also specifically consider the workload of struggling readers. And let's compare our kids' workload with that of regular-orthography kids.

Our crushed and crumpled koalas struggling with reading, writing and learning have a far higher workload than our healthy-progress readers. That's particularly the case for our bright kids with Language, Literacy and Learning Disorder (LLLD), who have major strengths and need to achieve good grades, in order to pursue university studies.

For them, life is tough in primary school and massively difficult in high school. High-school kids I work with have fortnightly sessions with me, plus 90 minutes home-practice weekly. On top of that, they take far longer than kids with strong literacy skills to do homework, because their reading and writing is slow and laborious, and assignments are too often a major ordeal, and take far longer to complete.

In addition, all too often our struggling readers are dragged through advanced learning they're simply not ready for, because they lack crucial basics. Again, that's particularly the case for high schoolers. Kids whose reading and spelling skills are years behind their classmates struggle enormously with required subject-area reading and writing, e.g., reading a text on the Roman Empire to summarise key points, and then write the class assignment.

Similarly, most kids not automatic on early maths skills endure too high cognitive load when working on later-years maths where complex calculations are needed.

Our kids with learning disability desperately need a well resourced and streamlined Australian Curriculum strand, which reduces subject-area time on literacy-heavy tasks, to enable the time needed for building essential basic skills.

John, who loves Maths and Science, would do streamlined History involving one less lesson per week. His class would watch a video on Douglas Mawson in the Antarctic then engage in a small-group discussion, whereas usual History classes would do extensive reading and writing. Ditto for Geography and Business.

Sarah, who loves Humanities, would do reduced Science, Japanese and Maths – and please don't think our current lower-level maths classes already offer this option, as many kids' numeracy skills are well below that level.

John and Sarah would then have three lessons per week of well-resourced Australian Curriculum learning support. They'd perhaps also do one less subject, to then have seven learning-support lessons each week. Strategically, the texts used in their learning support lessons would be on topics relevant to their subject-area learning, e.g., they'd read texts on Mawson and Antarctic exploration, year-level Science topics and practical Maths applications.

Once it's quantified, we'll be amazed by the workload our struggling readers endure, particularly our kids aiming for university, relative to both our healthy-progress kids, and lower-third kids in regular-orthography nations.

In weighing workload, let's also measure the workload and learning effectiveness of struggling readers, comparing it with the workload and learning effectiveness that the kids would have if our Australian Curriculum included multiple, impressively resourced, tailored curriculum strands for our at-risk and struggling learners.

Let's Weigh Child and Teacher Workload

Let's use hours of teaching and learning as a proxy for child and teacher workload. Logically, it's a reasonable way to think on workload, as work takes time.

We need to explore how hard our kids and teachers are working, how this relates to achievement outcomes, and how we compare with other nations.

Importantly, we also need to include measures of the effectiveness of that child and teacher workload, in terms of outcomes achieved by upper, middle and lower-third kids. Cost-benefit ratios are important.

There'd be value in exploring hours allocated to different subject areas, and the hours it takes upper, middle and lower-third kids to master different skills, to the level that regular-orthography thirds achieve. There's value too in exploring not just thirds but also finer groupings, including tenths, and the highest and lowest 5% and 2% of achievers.

Let's measure workload while linking it to kids' learning effectiveness: the teaching and learning time taken, plus the extent to which children have mastered that learning. We could do this for specific units of work taught here and in other nations, e.g., a novel study for Literature, a History unit on ancient Egypt, and a Science unit on rain.

Let's compare the hours our kids need for this learning, with the hours kids need in regular-orthography nations. Let's also measure how long it takes to master word-reading and spelling accuracy, in upper, middle and lower-third, and also our lowest-tenth kids.

We might monitor the ease and speed of kids' mastering of reading and spelling of sets of words with specific vowel and consonant combinations. Whereas regular-orthography Grade 1 kids can soon read and write virtually all words, our kids struggle with unfamiliar words of different types, with word-reading and spelling development sadly gradual.

For Maths, towards understanding big differences between our thirds of maths learners, as regards teaching and learning effectiveness, let's measure the time our thirds take to master the 2-times-tables well, understanding that e.g., 2x8 = 8x2 = 8+8 = double 8 = 16, plus using those maths skills effectively in practical maths applications.

I've deliberately picked 2-times-tables, as doubling is a key skill that's much needed in maths development, and also one which children with Language, Literacy and Learning Disorder (LLLD) often find extremely difficult to master.

It actually takes an enormous amount of time for many intelligent kids with learning difficulties to be automatic at counting down by 2s from 20, and the 2-times-tables. Many, if not most, high-school children I've worked with, lacked automaticity, e.g., struggled with sums such as 8 x 20.

In research studies assessing workload, it's also likely we'll explore the extent of stress and cognitive load that kids and teachers are experiencing. We'll perhaps use physiological measures, e.g., sweat levels, eye responses, and so on, as well as child and teacher surveys and interviews.

Let's be strategic in choosing which nations we'll compare ourselves with, then ask politely, towards building win-win collaborative research projects. In addition to Anglophone nations, let's also include at least one highly-regular sole-orthography GENTLE nation, such as Finland or Estonia.

And let's insist we ask nations such as Taiwan and Japan to work with us – role-model nations that use highly-regular orthographies initially, to expedite early-literacy, and then transition kids to their complex orthography.

Let's Weigh Our Find the Learning Time Challenge

When I sit in classrooms in regular-orthography nations observing teaching and learning, and talk with teachers, I don't perceive the stress of our schools – the relentless pressure our kids and teachers live with as schools struggle to fit in all the teaching and learning that must be done.

Despite us spending far more hours in the classroom, our schools emanate the stress of time-pressure: our chronic Find the Learning Time Challenge and Find the Caring Time Challenge. This pressures our children and teachers, and markedly reduces teaching and learning effectiveness.

Schools in all nations need teaching hours for subject-area learning: Maths, Science, History, Geography, Humanities, and so on. So too do we.

Where Anglophone nations differ is in the additional mega-hours we must use, to build kids' word-reading and spelling skills, and support our developing and struggling readers.

That will likely prove our biggest workload factor relative to regular-orthography nations.

School hours are finite, and time allocated to word-reading and spelling development and supporting fledgling literacy skills reduces time for subject-area teaching and learning.

While our school hours are too long, they're clearly not long enough for the massive workload we have from using solely Standard English without a beginners' orthography. Given our sadly low education outcomes, the extra 300 hours each year clearly doesn't compensate for our excessive early-literacy workload.

Using solely Standard English, it's likely we'd use at least a thousand or so teaching and learning hours developing word-reading and spelling at school and in homework, then likely at least a thousand or so more hours supporting kids' slowly-developing literacy skills in subject-area learning. That's particularly the case, given that perhaps a third of our high-schoolers are struggling readers.

Most definitely, we do not want to increase our school hours further. We instead need to reduce the early-literacy workload that creates need for those long hours. This creates strong value in 10 Changes improvements, which drastically reduce early-literacy workload and effort.

Regular-orthography nations spend only a tiny fraction of the time we do on word-reading and spelling instruction, and supporting developing and struggling readers.

Let's explore how they save time and spend it, while we measure workload and work hours.

In measuring child and teacher workload here and in other nations, let's also focus on the number and proportion of hours that are allocated to

- Developing early-literacy skills.
- Subject-area learning.
- Supporting developing readers in subject-area learning.
- Supporting struggling readers in all learning areas.

Let's Weigh Our Education Habits

Let's also weigh the impacts of some education habits which are more specifically Australian, including

- How we action and resource disability *Inclusion*.
- Our excessive primary-school testing.
- Our excessive primary-school report-card writing.
- Primary-school teachers changing classes every year.
- Our low extent of teaching resources provided by our Australian Curriculum developers.
- Our too high teacher administration duties.
- Our needs for increased learning supports.
- Our needs for increased allied-health supports.

Inclusion and Its Resourcing

Inclusion is schools including children with disabilities of varying severity in mainstream primary and high-school classes. It's excellent in many ways, however, to work well, it needs to be resourced extremely well, otherwise class-teacher workload can be heightened excessively.

Inclusion works well here for many children, however the resourcing provided for their education is often insufficient. It also seems the case that our highly experienced teachers often have highest numbers of severely struggling learners.

When class-teacher resourcing for Inclusion is inadequate, this can reduce teaching and learning effectiveness for all kids, both disabled and non-disabled alike.

It's interesting that PIRLS and PISA studies don't include Inclusion and its resourcing as impacting factors that they explore. That's a bunyip. Quite likely, our heightened class-teacher workload due to insufficiently resourced Inclusion, coupled with low resourcing generally, lowers our results relative to those nations that don't have Inclusion. It's also possibly reflected in our PISA pattern of fewer high achievers and increasingly more low achievers.

There seems value in measuring the extent to which Inclusion heightens teacher workload, and the resourcing needed so that our teachers' workload for Inclusion kids is no higher than their workload, on average, for all kids.

Primary School Testing and Report Cards

Strategic assessment can be valuable, showing both how well children are doing, and their instructional needs for future teaching.

That said, time spent testing is time not spent teaching, thus there's value in finding the right balance between too little and too much testing.

Many leading nations don't do nearly our extent of end-of-term testing, data analysis and reporting in primary school. In addition, their teachers seem somewhat horrified by our extent of primary-school testing. Is that a bunyip for you?

In our schools' rush to get through our extensive Australian Curriculum content, then do testing then reporting, our teachers don't have the time they'd need to learn from their kids' results and adjust instruction accordingly.

In addition, results often strongly align with what teacher estimates would be without that testing. Further, for struggling readers, subject-area test results often reflect their weak literacy, rather than their subject-area learning.

Testing and report-card writing also add exhaustingly to teacher workload. Too many teachers work too many long hours, late at night and on weekends and holidays, setting and marking tests, and writing report cards.

Cost-benefit analyses will likely show our cute koalas and their teachers obtain grossly-insufficient benefit from the extensive testing and reporting our primary schools do.

Certainly, there's value in us weighing the workload of our primary-school testing, data usage and reporting habits, relative to the assessment habits of other nations.

There's also value in considering the reasons for our habits. Quite likely it's because early-literacy development here is such a struggle, with improvement more Titanic style, while early-literacy and improvement are, for the most part, both thriving, racing-yacht style, in regular-orthography nations.

Teachers Changing Classes Every Year

In other nations, it's common for primary-school teachers to teach children for up to three years, e.g., with kids having one teacher for Grades 1 to 3, and another for later grades. That's perhaps a bunyip.

In Australia, our habit is kids having a new teacher every year. There's every likelihood this reduces effectiveness of teaching and learning. For a start, it takes much of Term 1 for teachers to build thorough understanding of each child. Then, teaching time is lost in Term 4, when there's a sense of wind-down and getting ready for fond farewells.

In contrast, when kids and teachers know they'll have the Christmas holidays then continue work as usual, much is gained, and workload is often considerably reduced.

We Aussies worry about personality clashes if kids had the same teacher for two to three years, so I asked about this when visiting schools in regular-orthography nations.

No, personality clashes are not an issue, and they were very surprised I asked. Instead, families and teachers know each other well and support each other very effectively.

Perhaps our thoughts of personality clashes relate more to our education woes generally, with our schools having far too many stressed teachers juggling excessive work demands and struggling readers whose needs aren't adequately met.

Teachers, families and kids in regular-orthography nations find teachers taking the same class for several years works well for all kids, including weaker and advanced learners, who can more easily receive tailoring of learning.

We really do need to weigh the workload value of our habit of primary-school teachers changing classes each year.

Needs for National Curriculum Materials

Many nations have far more specific detail in their national curricula than we do. They also have year-level textbooks and student workbooks for each subject-area, with teachers often knowing the precise content they'll teach each week, and parents able to know this too. More bunyips.

Now while we Aussies might be concerned at the level of control involved, it's interesting that teachers in regular-orthography nations don't feel that way. They appreciate the precision provided. Professional development and mentoring is focused on honing teaching of individual lessons and units, far more than happens here, so kids master content more easily and effectively. Another bunyip.

In Australian schools, our teachers are usually too busy to do that highly-specific honing. They are additionally busy because our Australian Curriculum doesn't provide our schools with well-developed curriculum units and resources. This increases workload markedly, and the wheel is reinvented endlessly across our schools, as teachers in each school develop curriculum and resources, year after year.

Certainly, even if not compulsory, there seem advantages to curriculum units being developed at national level, along with resourcing for units, including strategic activities for advanced and struggling learners at a range of skill levels.

There's indeed value in weighing the workload associated with national-curriculum specificity and resourcing, here and in regular-orthography nations that have far more specified and well-resourced national curricula.

Heightened Teacher Administration Duties

Let's weigh the amount of administration our teachers do now, comparing it with the amount done 10 and 20 years ago, and the extent that we've adjusted teachers' workloads, to accommodate this increased administrative workload.

With litigation having proliferated across the decades, our teachers do masses of administration for all kids, then far more for struggling readers and learners. Records are kept, meetings held, and individual program forms completed. There's now further Nationally Consistent Collection of Data (NCCD) workload, with our teachers gathering data on all their struggling learners and their support needs.

For many struggling readers and learners, it seems we've mastered the administrative requirements of tailoring their education, with teachers completing detailed documents. But we then fail at the classroom coalface, where the rich education detailed in those documents is severely lacking, due to too high workloads and too low school resourcing.

Emails and texts to parents, collectively and individually, also seem now a required teacher service. They take time, as teachers often write quite cautiously.

Our teachers don't command the respect they had 20 years ago, which teachers in leading regular-orthography nations still enjoy – and, at some time, virtually all our teachers have unhappily endured tirades from upset parents.

Consequently, in written communications, our teachers are understandably cautious in their wording, carefully proofing to ensure they've not said what might be misconstrued.

They're similarly careful in what they say to parents in meetings, interviews and chats before and after school. This all takes time and effort.

Administration work for excursions is now of monumental proportions. The legal protections schools need to take kids on camps and excursions have proliferated the forms that must be completed, and the hours spent chasing up those needed forms, so kids aren't left out.

Sadly, potential litigation means our cute koala kids miss out in many ways, e.g., there seem far fewer excursions, particularly the tiny informal outings of decades past, with relevant lessons conducted at the local beach or park.

Yes, our teachers now have masses of administration, and there's been insufficient workload adjustment to offset their extra work. This contributes to our teachers being far too busy to provide the effective teaching they're so capable of.

Needs for Learning and Allied-Health Supports

In measuring child and teacher workload, let's assess our lower-third learners, and estimate the accommodations and intervention needed for them to receive the rich education that our Education Act promises.

Let's assess the adequacy of the intervention and supports currently received. As an example, it's disappointing that, at least in some states, our learning-support teachers are often class-teachers who've not been provided needed additional training. This contrasts markedly with many nations where Masters-level qualifications are required.

In a nation that proliferates our kids' literacy difficulties by starting word-reading and spelling of one of the world's most complex orthographies at close to the world's youngest age, we need exemplary expertise in learning-support, to prevent and overcome difficulties. Our not prioritising expertise for learning-support is therefore a very distressing bunyip.

Further, our learning-support teachers are often far too busy with administration duties, to the extent that one-to-one support sessions are often rare, and numbers in supposedly *small-group* intervention are all too often regrettably large.

Our teacher aides so often do most of our learning support, and all too often their *small* groups have eight to 10 crushed and crumpled koalas, not two to three. More bunyips.

Our teacher aides are wonderful supports in education here, but most feel they'd be far more effective if they were provided with systematic training and mentoring. They'd love to be guided by highly-trained, expert learning-support teachers; to have time to provide lots more one-on-one support; and to have groups of two to three kids whom they work with frequently, so real progress can be achieved.

Our schools' learning-support systems are thus, in many cases, far from adequate. Let's measure our children's needs, current services and workloads, and what's needed for us to provide far more optimal learning support.

Of course, class-teacher workload is intricately related to learning-support workload and efficiency, as class teachers must provide the missing supports, when school learning-support and allied-health supports are insufficient.

Our research might use panels of GPs, paediatricians, and allied-health professionals in private practice, who are highly experienced in providing support and intervention to Aussie kids with learning struggles, and their families.

Using data on kids' achievement levels for, e.g., reading comprehension, subject-area learning, language skills and word-reading; and samples of kids' written work; these panels would estimate the adequacy of current supports; and the extent of future supports that the kids need from class teachers, learning-support teachers, teacher aides and allied-health professionals.

Let's Weigh NAPLAN Bullying and Attribution Error

Let's also measure the workload and stress impacts of what is often termed *NAPLAN bullying* and *teacher bashing* – pressure from politicians, journalists, education systems and families on our schools and teachers, insisting they improve reading outcomes and education generally.

Let's also measure the impact of attribution error – our inappropriately blaming one factor as the cause of a problem, while ignoring other key causal factors involved.

Attribution error has been rampant in education here.

Our bullies blame poor teaching, positioning it as virtually the sole cause of our education struggles.

However, the teaching that our teachers achieve in current circumstances is a far-lesser causal factor than many others.

More pertinent causal factors include
- Child factors, e.g., many kids start primary school too at-risk of learning difficulties, and far too many start high school with woefully insufficient literacy skills.
- Systemic factors, e.g., insufficient resourcing for early-literacy learning, too few skilled learning-support teachers and teacher aides, and too meagre allied-health supports prior to and across the school years.
- Orthographic disadvantage factors, e.g., many kids being too immature for the complex learning of Standard English, our too slow early-literacy development, our excessive workload, our too many severely struggling readers, our too busy teachers and our Find the Learning Time Challenge.

Unfortunately, NAPLAN bullying has had massive impacts on teacher workload, through schools adopting excessive numbers of school improvement initiatives in response. These can't be highly effective, as they heighten teacher busyness, and then the law of diminishing returns applies.

There's value in measuring how our teachers' workload has increased through NAPLAN bullying and the improvement initiatives actioned in our schools. There's also value in measuring how effective those initiatives have been, and the extent of stress and anxiety they've engendered.

Let's also measure the extent our education systems have worked to improve education by reducing and mitigating the impacts of child, resourcing and orthography factors.

NAPLAN bullying has also included NAPLAN results being used punitively, with teachers and schools made to feel inadequate and judged by their NAPLAN results. That's an utter nonsense, really, given
- More-expert teachers often having more kids with complex needs in their classes.
- Schools with a reputation for providing learning supports often having more struggling readers.

- Large numbers of kids changing schools, with their teaching impacts thus shared across schools.
- Child, system and orthographic complexity factors.

Unfortunately, NAPLAN bullying and its companion, our insufficient school resourcing to support at-risk kids from start of school, have resulted in many schools and teachers loathing NAPLAN, and calling for its end.

That's sad. NAPLAN is a reasonably efficient system that will become both more efficient and more useful for schools as online differentiated, responsive testing evolves; and we have far less national testing than, e.g., many USA states.

I consider NAPLAN a keeper – we benefit from seeing how our kids and schools are going over time.

While it may not show in NAPLAN results, our schools and teachers are now considerably stronger at building reading-comprehension, genre and written-expression skills. What we measure, we often manage more effectively, and when our teachers see areas of need they can improve, they work hard to do so, and achieve improved learning.

What's needed is for NAPLAN nastiness to stop, along with attribution error that ridiculously says improving teaching is all we need, to achieve heightened learning and results.

Let's take the blame out of NAPLAN. Let's also get NAPLAN results back faster to schools, as useful feedback to guide instruction. At present, delayed NAPLAN feedback and teachers changing classes every year are a very poor combination.

Let's also remove the stress schools feel before NAPLAN, and the pressured teaching and learning they sometimes feel they need to do. Let's make NAPLAN simply a usual routine part of schooling, one that provides our education systems with indicators of annual resourcing needed.

Let's end the judgement and pressure that's currently our norm. Results will then show how well things are going, with low results logically being education-system outcomes easily as much as school outcomes.

They'd show the effectiveness of current resourcing, and also the extent of increased learning support and allied-health resourcing that's needed for individual kids and schools.

In addition, Year 3 NAPLAN results would be an estimate of the effectiveness of current early-years education and resourcing from start of school, and show the extent to which greater supports are needed.

Let's Weigh Resourcing

Supports provided for teaching and learning impact child and teacher workload in both direct and indirect ways.

These supports include teacher time on-class and off-class, and hours of support from teacher-aides, learning-support teachers and allied-health professionals. They also include teacher's time release, teacher-aide time for administrative duties, and national-curriculum specificity and resourcing.

These supports can, in effect, create time for class teachers, and reduce their total workload. They potentially enable more effective class teaching through teachers not always working under pressure and being close to overwhelmed.

Resourcing also includes technology supports that reduce teacher and child workload, e.g., every classroom having highly effective assistive technology. At the time that I'm writing, this should include

- Computers, document cameras, interactive whiteboards and effective internet access.
- Teacher microphones linked to room speakers, so every child can hear the teacher clearly.
- Speech-to-text software and text-to-speech scanners enabling faster, easier reading and writing.

Specialist teachers for specific subjects are also resourcing. Many primary-school teachers here don't teach Music and Health and Physical Education (HPE), and have off-class time while specialist teachers teach those subjects. This reduces class-teacher workload by removing preparation and administration time, and increasing off-class time.

Other nations take this further in strategic ways, e.g., in Taiwanese primary schools, specialist teachers also teach Art and Science. While reducing class-teacher workload, this also positions class teachers as specialist literacy and Maths teachers, who focus on heightening their expertise for teaching these subjects.

Student-free time is also resourcing. It's used for meetings, year-level discussions, one-on-one work with students, mentoring, the many compliance courses teachers must complete (e.g., fire safety, child protection, diabetes training, anaphylaxis training, and workplace health and safety), professional development – and so much more. Our teachers and schools are busy, that's for sure.

Australian schools struggle to fit all that's needed into meagre student-free days, and some schools even divide these up into multiple, exhausting, *twilight sessions* tacked onto the end of busy school days.

In contrast, teachers in other nations have vastly more off-class time for school duties. Every Wednesday in Taiwan, school finishes at lunchtime, with the afternoons used for professional development, meetings and administration.

Additionally, many nations, e.g., Estonia, have the option of student-free weeks across the long summer break. Most schools don't use them as education is going well, however the contrast of our struggles to find sufficient student-free time with the ready availability of time in other nations is quite staggering. Bunyips, anyone?

Yes, resourcing takes many and varied forms. And clearly, in weighing workload, there's value in measuring the types and amounts of resourcing provided here and elsewhere.

How Much Time Does It Take?

It's important to realise that, with our schools having continued so long with too low resourcing, we don't actually know the extent of resourcing our schools need to optimise learning to read and write for our at-risk and struggling readers. Now, that's a very sad bunyip.

No one seems to have calculated the resourcing needed for us to effectively support our weaker learners, to get their reading and writing skills to class level and keep them there.

Partly, that's because few, and perhaps no, schools are effective in achieving this. We've quite a few bunyips here.

Studies show Standard-English kids' word-reading levels in Grade 1 predict both their literacy skills and academic achievement generally in later primary and high school.

Other studies show that most struggling Standard English word-readers do make gains, but all too often they don't maintain those gains, or catch up to healthy progress and stay there.

Our struggling readers seem entitled to at least year-level word-reading and spelling skills, if they're to achieve the education we promise them, given that these skills are acquired so easily by regular-orthography weaker readers.

It's Swiss-cheese research time, and we've major needs for learning from useful, practical, future research.

Needed: Four Strategic Additions

Our children are our future. Our strongest investment in their education is thus our schools and teachers, and the quality of teaching they can provide. It's therefore pivotal that we empower our teachers, schools and teaching.

I'll list here four key resourcing items our schools need if kids in all of our thirds are to have an effective education.

Item 1. Reduced Class-Teaching Hours

First up, let's reduce annual class-teaching hours for our teachers, to Finland's sensible 677 hours, setting that as our maximum. On average, our teachers would gain at least 200 hours administration time annually: five hours in each of our 40 school weeks, one extra hour per day. Currently, on its own, this extra resourcing would be merely a token gesture, given our teachers' busyness, but it's a useful start.

Item 2. One Full-Time Teacher Aide for Every Teacher

Second, let's change to every class teacher having a full-time teacher aide, who works strategically with kids in the classroom, and on administration tasks.

Each class teacher having a teacher aide would make an enormous difference for our teachers and kids. Our cute koalas would get considerably more individual attention, tailored instruction would be more the norm, and teachers' administrative workload would be appreciably reduced.

Of course, that full-time teacher-aide for each class teacher would be additional to teacher-aide time allocated for children with identified disabilities.

Together those two resourcing changes have potential to improve teaching and learning somewhat.

Item 3. Increased Supports for At-Risk Children

For considerably stronger teaching and learning, let's also add a desperately-needed resourcing change – the supports our lower-third kids need to achieve successful education.

Let's add in additional learning-support teachers, teacher aides, and school allied-health supports to a level that will definitely improve the education our kids receive.

We've far too many kids with major language weakness, and excessive numbers of struggling readers and learners.

Until education is achieving well for our lower-third and lowest-tenth, there are compelling grounds for us greatly increasing intervention resourcing, particularly given our Education Act emphasises that this should be provided.

From my thorough knowledge of our struggling readers' support needs and the gross inadequacy of the school supports they currently receive, I see very strong grounds for greatly increased resourcing.

It's likely, towards achieving major improvement, that all Australian primary schools and high schools should be allocated, for every 500 enrolled children in their schools,

- One highly-skilled learning-support teacher with Masters-level qualifications, and four well-trained learning-support teacher aides.
- One speech language pathologist with education training, and four communication aides.
- One occupational therapist with education training, with four occupational therapy aides.
- One social worker with education training.
- One psychologist with education training.

Item 4. National Curriculum Supports

Let's also ensure that our Australian Curriculum is as streamlined and amply resourced as the national curricula of leading nations, e.g., of nations such as Finland, Estonia, Taiwan, Japan and China.

Further, let's insist it includes streamlined options for our cute koala kids with learning disability, and for extending our high-progress learners.

Let's also have national curriculum textbooks, workbooks and associated teaching materials for all subjects in each year-level, not necessarily compulsory but there as useful options. It's time to end the wheel being reinvented endlessly, ad nauseum, as individual Aussie schools and teachers develop curriculum and resources that would be better provided at Australian Curriculum level.

Let's make sure these teaching materials prioritise strategic differentiation and are amply resourced, so teachers find them extremely useful, and strong supports for

- Skilled teaching of year-level learning.
- Remediating and supporting of weaker learners.
- Extending of advanced learners.

Let's also ensure that strategic remedial and advanced resources are included for every subject-area unit, to accommodate and remediate weak word-reading, writing and learning.

Together, those four improvements would make a highly meaningful difference to the education all our kids receive.

They're greatly needed, and perhaps even crucial, if we're to achieve significant improvement.

Expensive, you say? Most definitely!

Needed? Most definitely! Australian education is going to be considerably more costly until we're improving well.

Excessive? Most definitely not.

I know well the instructional needs of our lower-third and lowest-tenth struggling readers. We need at least these four additions if we're to achieve effective education. We'll need them for as long as we stick to solely Standard English and kids aged 4.5 to 5 years when learning to read and write.

We've chosen a hugely-expensive spelling system, and are managing its complexity very poorly. In consequence, it's crushing too many cute koalas, our teachers and education generally. We have then exacerbated our difficulties by inadequately resourcing our schools.

We've too frequently paid the high costs of orthographic disadvantage in the sufferings of our struggling readers and their teachers.

It's time to redress the balance and fund the supports needed to move our kids and teachers from HEARTSH to GENTLE, and from survive to thrive.

Change 3: Weigh Workload

Change 3 is important for our progress: *Weigh workload: Our children and teachers are working far too hard.*

Let's measure workload, and gather facts and data on how hard our kids and teachers work relative to kids and teachers in other nations. Workload is far too much a Swiss-cheese area at present – almost all gaps, no cheese.

Our schools currently spend perhaps thousands more hours supporting our kids' reading and spelling development, at school and in homework, than regular-orthography nations, while still needing to achieve strong subject-area learning.

This slog of additional hours means our kids and teachers' workloads are far too high, plus the massive needs of our too many struggling readers add additional, unacceptably-high, teacher workload.

We've currently too much work spread across too few adults, and our teachers can't do Superman on a daily and weekly basis. By reducing class-teaching hours; increasing our teacher, teacher-aide and allied-health numbers; and also increasing our Australian Curriculum supports and teaching resources; we'll strategically reduce the excessive workload our teachers wrestle with. That will be a strong positive investment in improving education here.

There's every likelihood that the law of diminishing returns undermines all our improvement efforts.

When our teachers are forced to work too hard, teaching effectiveness reduces. When kids are tired from too many school hours, and unmotivated due to receiving insufficient mentoring, learning effectiveness similarly dwindles.

We desperately need to weigh child and teacher workload, doing the research needed to explore this area thoroughly.

Both our children and our teachers are struggling badly, and need gentler, more effective education. Our teachers are our biggest investment in education yet currently we're crushing them. It's imperative that we strategically improve the supports we provide.

Towards improving education here, we need to strategically weigh child and teacher workload, gathering important information so we've detailed knowledge of how hard kids and teachers are working across nations, and what constitutes a healthy, manageable workload.

That will give us a strong basis for considering how we can achieve healthy workload as part of improving education.

Change 4
Respect Learning Differences

Findings revealed that specific patterns of instructional activities differentially predicted [Grade 1] children's decoding skill:
(a) Children with low initial decoding scores achieved greater decoding growth in classrooms with more time spent in teacher-managed explicit decoding instruction. In contrast, for children with initially high decoding scores, amount of teacher-managed explicit decoding had no effect ...
(b) Children with high initial vocabulary scores achieved greater decoding growth in classrooms with more time spent in child-managed implicit activities.

Carol McDonald Connor et al.[xxvii], 2004

Change 4 states, *One-size education does not fit all: Teach to the decidedly different instructional needs of upper-third and lower-third readers.*

Those of us who are good readers acquired early-literacy skills quite easily. Because of this, we may not appreciate just how incredibly difficult it can be for our struggling Standard English readers to learn to read and write.

There are actually very big differences in the learning and cognitive-processing skills of our high-achieving upper-third readers and our struggling lower-third readers. These in turn create big differences in their instructional needs.

Those instructional differences are important.

Let's build understanding of those differences. One size instruction does not fit all, particularly while we stick to solely Standard English. Let's tailor instruction so it usefully meets our cute koalas' individual needs.

Change 4 contrasts our upper and lower-third readers. Of course, middle-third kids are equally important, and it's likely we'd simultaneously study all three thirds of kids.

However, the contrast of our upper-third and lower-third in their development of different literacy skills is particularly powerful for providing insights and knowledge into how kids' instructional needs differ and how we can best meet those needs. This contrast can produce powerful knowledge on how to best hone instruction for all three thirds of kids.

Tokenism and Teaching to the Middle

When it comes to key teaching and learning differences between our upper and lower-third readers, Australian education is often guilty of tokenism. That's a bunyip.

We say we tailor instruction to meet individual children's needs, but too often this smacks of rhetoric, particularly when our teachers are so busy.

We need every class teacher to be efficiently and effectively
- Extending our upper-third higher achievers.
- Teaching and empowering our middle-third.
- Remediating our lower-third, while providing them with comprehensive subject-area learning.

Those are teaching facts of life we all know well.

Unfortunately, to cover our copious Australian Curriculum content plus keep teaching manageable, while also developing curriculum and resources, our teachers often end up teaching to the middle – because they're too busy. They teach the required content to all students, but aren't able to effectively extend their upper-third students, or provide the remediation and accommodations that their lower-third students need.

This leads to one-size-fits-all instruction, which definitely does not fit all when it comes to the learning strengths, weaknesses and instructional needs of our upper and lower-third cute koala kids.

That's not a criticism I'm making – that's life in a nation that inadequately supports its teachers and our struggling readers, and where students' estimation of their school experience positions us as eighth worst in the world for unruly classrooms.

Teaching in Australia is indeed a very tough job. Quite likely, too frequent survival-mode teaching to the middle underlies our steady PISA trend of our numbers of high achievers falling as our numbers of low achievers rise.

Thirds, Busyness and Our Reading Wars

There's every likelihood that our difficulties achieving effectively differentiated instruction contribute strongly to our ongoing Reading Wars – ongoing divisiveness about the extent to which word-reading is important and should be systematically taught and tested.

One side, whom we might term *Word-Reading Scientists*, considers the needs of all children, but is especially focused on lower-third word-readers and their instructional needs, concerned that weak readers' needs are being overlooked. Their actions reflect this focus.

They're right, of course.

The other side, whom we might term *Literacy-Enrichment Advocates*, is concerned that the language and literacy enrichment of our cute koala kids might be overlooked or omitted if too much instructional focus and time is spent on word-reading instruction.

Of course, they're right, as well.

In many ways, they're taking more of an upper-third perspective. Additionally, most have seen more than a few struggling readers for whom schools' systematic word-reading instruction worked poorly (which happens all too often in our inadequately resourced, time-poor schools). Consequently, some question the efficacy of systematic word-reading instruction as a whole.

Importantly, all might be easily resolved if we could have what both sides would love: time to have it all – time for both effective individualised instruction that provides the needed amount of appropriate word-reading instruction, and time for extensive language and literacy enrichment.

In that sense of wanting to have it all, our Word-Reading Scientists and Literacy Enrichment Advocates think very similarly. Both groups would like systematic word-reading instruction to the extent kids need and would benefit from, and both would like extensive literacy enrichment.

Alas, unlike regular-orthography nations, we unfortunately don't have time for both. That's a very sad bunyip.

Our Reading Wars are a time-pressure issue. That's a bunyip too.

Our divisiveness builds from our schools' Find the Learning Time Challenge and our complex curriculum conundrum of having too much to teach in too little time, and too many crumpled koalas who are seriously struggling readers.

Amidst that pressure, there's no way we can have it all. Consequently both factions correctly continue to view the situation as immensely unsatisfactory, and argue strongly for their priorities.

Regular-orthography nations achieve having it all because their kids need so little instructional time to master word-reading and spelling, thus making their schools time-rich.

In contrast, here and in other Anglophone nations, Reading Wars divisiveness is perpetuated by the too high workload and time-pressure that English orthographic complexity creates. This denies us having it all and results in us not sufficiently achieving either of systematic word-reading instruction or ample literacy enrichment.

Thus our Reading Wars continue.

Now here's an interesting bunyip. There's every likelihood that Whole Language advocates of the 1960s not embracing the Initial Teaching Alphabet (ITA) or a similar fully-regular English beginners' orthography, will prove to be the Anglosphere's greatest education tragedy ever.

Together, Whole Language and ITA would have been an absolute winner. We'd effortlessly have been able to have it all, with our kids revelling in the joy of literacy and learning. That's because we'd have been time-rich, with early literacy happening easily and quite effortlessly, and very few kids having major literacy difficulties. Yes, we'd have had ample time for literacy and learning enrichment down the decades.

We need to resolve our Reading Wars challenges. We can do that best by improving education so we too are time-rich due to rapid, easy early-literacy.

Most definitely, the 10 Changes offer impressive potential for Australia leaving divisiveness behind and achieving that wonderful all.

As part of this, we need to establish the different strengths and needs of our upper and lower-third readers.

Research Establishes Definite Differences

To clarify learning differences, let's build understanding of the different instructional needs of upper and lower-third kids for optimal development of specific skills, including word-reading, spelling, language and thinking, vocabulary, reading comprehension and written-expression skills.

International research gives us good news. Studies clearly show that upper and lower-third word-readers have very different instructional needs, and both need their specific requirements catered to, to make effective progress.

Different Literacy Instructional Needs
The Research Tours discusses some excellent USA research that's explored the different instructional needs of successful and unsuccessful Standard English readers.

It's now very well established that the balance of reading instruction needs to be tweaked in different directions for upper and lower-third kids as regards the amounts of systematic word-reading instruction and meaning-based instruction they receive.

Upper-third, strong-progress word-readers need only a small amount of explicit word-reading instruction, and can fail to thrive in classrooms where lots of time is spent on word-reading skills. They need and benefit from ample meaning-based reading and writing, and make excellent progress when this is provided, with their teachers often taking the role of facilitators of learning, giving kids what they need.

Lower-third word-readers don't progress nearly as well when instruction is mostly meaning-based.

Whilst they definitely need meaningful reading and writing, they make far greater progress when also provided with considerable systematic word-reading instruction, and lots of fun practice that helps them develop the confident word-reading skills they need for healthy literacy progress.

They also make significantly poorer progress when that systematic instruction isn't provided.

Lower-third word-readers also need effective emotional supports and encouragement if they're to progress. Studies show they do less well in classes that have strong word-reading instruction but lack emotional supports.

The research of Carol McDonald Connor and colleagues is powerful, providing practical useful findings on differing instructional needs. Do visit their *Individualising Student Instruction* website (isilearn.net), and read their research articles. The team's focus is on cooperative research, with schools joining in and using the researchers' provided resources, with schools then sharing their de-identified data on their kids' achievement levels and progress. Schools' data, in turn, contributes to ongoing research studies.

It's an eminently practical research model which is very much win-win. It would be very powerful for Australian education to join that research, or to set up collaborative research studies across Australia which similarly explore these areas.

Different Cognitive Processing Levels

Our thirds also have distinct differences when it comes to key cognitive-processing skills, which underlie learning efficiency. These skills include short-term and working memory, processing speed, storing information in long-term memory and retrieving it efficiently, automising skills, and orthographic, phonological and phonemic awareness.

Our thirds also differ on executive-function skills used in reading and learning tasks: skills used in maintaining focused attention, planning, self-monitoring, evaluating and prioritising information and time usage, and actioning and appraising tasks through to completion. Executive-function skills are pivotal for Standard English literacy and learning, when a beginners' orthography isn't used.

Different Statistical Learning Levels

Marked differences between our thirds are also the case for what's termed *statistical learning*: learning by noticing patterns in what we encounter, either implicitly or as part of explicit teaching and learning.

Statistical learning is how, as littlies, we all learned to speak and use sentences of increasing maturity. It's also to a large extent how kids learn to read and write. Statistical learning can be implicit (done without adult help), explicit (using strategic explanations and scaffolded practice), or both.

Regular-orthography kids do strongest statistical learning. It's unimpeded because there's so little confusion, and thus they develop word-reading and spelling quickly and easily. In contrast, our kids must wend their way through massive orthographic confusion that markedly impedes statistical learning, e.g., the conflicting vowel sounds they encounter in otherwise highly-similar words such as n*o*t/n*ow* w*as*/h*as*, *one*/b*one*, g*o*/d*o*, g*one*/d*one*, c*a*n/c*a*r, t*o*p/t*oy*, s*i*t/s*i*r.

While far weaker than regular-orthography kids, upper-third Standard English word-readers are relatively strong statistical learners – they both manage and learn from the orthographic confusion they encounter. That's why they need less systematic word-reading instruction, and benefit so much from engaged reading and writing.

In contrast, our lower-third word-readers are usually poor statistical learners for early-literacy skills and concepts. They're easily overwhelmed by the confusion that upper-third readers find interesting and stimulating.

That's why lower-third readers benefit so much more from systematic, explicit word-reading instruction with lots of scaffolded practice, as this reduces confusion and promotes much stronger statistical learning.

Our kids' much weaker statistical learning and slow, drawn-out word-reading and spelling development, are important reasons why we need to explore the use of fully-regular beginners' orthographies, used prior to Standard English – because beginners' orthographies produce strong statistical learning in all three thirds of learners.

The Balance of Self-Teaching and Resourcing Needs

We've also marked differences in self-teaching skills between our upper and lower-thirds, and our kids and regular-orthography kids. Self-teaching, our kids' skills for teaching themselves to read and write unfamiliar words without outside help, can powerfully expedite learning.

As word-reading skills and confidence build, kids are increasingly able to self-teach. Pleasingly, as self-teaching skills and confidence increase, kids need less adult help.

That's why Japanese Grade 1 classes have 37 children, and why 1960s teachers using ITA were time-rich, and better able to tailor teaching and learning.

Self-teaching is thus directly related to schools' resourcing needs, in addition to being an important aspect of kids becoming stronger, increasingly-independent word-readers, spellers, readers, writers and learners.

Having stronger self-teaching, our upper-third kids become independent readers and writers more quickly. They soon need less and less adult support, and progress well through doing ample meaningful reading and writing.

Lower-third kids, in contrast, have delayed development of both skills and self-teaching, and all too often need adult support. They need skilful building of word-reading skills that eases them into increasingly-confident word-reading, self-teaching, and independence in reading and writing.

Acquired Helplessness Vs Success Inoculation

Acquired Helplessness and *Success Inoculation* will likely prove to be important factors separating the easy education of regular-orthography nations from our orthographic disadvantage and education woes. They're bunyips too.

Acquired Helplessness, which is widely known as *Learned Helplessness*, is subdued, depressed behaviour we move into when we don't feel capable of doing a task, but can't escape it. We hence endure it, often passively waiting for the activity to end, rather than actively engaging in it.

Maier and Seligman, who originated Learned Helplessness theory in the 1960s, decided this helplessness was learned. They've since realised, through multiple studies, that it is success that has learned impacts, while helplessness is almost unavoidable when initial learning involves ongoing low success. They've since revised Learned Helplessness theory. In their 2016 article, *Learned Helplessness at 50: Insights from Neuroscience*, they state[xxviii],

> *The mechanism of learned helplessness is now very well-charted biologically, and the original theory got it backward. Passivity in response to shock is not learned. It is the default, unlearned response to prolonged aversive events.*

In our CQU research team's writing, we contrast Acquired Helplessness and its passive behaviours, with Success Inoculation – the resilience learners acquire when they experience vigorous success.

It's highly likely that Success Inoculation and Acquired Helplessness produce corresponding positive and negative changes in children's cognitive-processing and executive-function skills, thus impacting their learning and progress.

Logically, and yet another bunyip, there's every likelihood that major differences exist in their impacts on our lower and upper-third word-readers, and also in their impacts on our children compared to regular-orthography children.

It's Swiss-cheese research time, as there's amazingly little research on Acquired Helplessness and Success Inoculation in word-reading development.

Their effects quite likely heighten differences in statistical learning, self-teaching and learning generally. They'll prove to be key factors in our lower and upper-third's differences in Standard English word-reading and early-literacy skills.

It's also likely that our Find the Learning Time Challenge and Find the Caring Time Challenge exacerbate Acquired Helplessness and its effects.

The Widening Divide

Kids' cognitive-processing efficiency underlies their literacy learning efficiency. We thus see much faster learning progress in upper-third readers, and much slower progress in our lower-third strugglers – in effect, a widening divide.

The Kinder Upper-Third Life

By our standards, our upper-third children master word-reading and spelling to a sufficient level quite quickly, becoming relatively-confident, independent readers and writers. They then perpetuate their progress by engaging in lots of reading and writing, and becoming increasingly effective self-teachers.

With strong cognitive-processing skills, and their working memory expanded by confidence, they are very soon primarily focused on meaning, taking in and reflecting on the content of what they read, and transferring their thinking into writing. With few risk factors, they don't just survive but even thrive across the Early Years Factory journey, enjoying the successes they experience every day.

Life is kind to them too, as they're unaware that they're sadly slow learners compared to regular-orthography kids.

The Sad Lower-Third Life

In sad contrast to our confident upper-third word-readers, our lower-third cute koalas come to school laden with risk factors, which are then activated by Standard English and the high cognitive load of learning to read and write.

With phonological and phonemic awareness and reading-readiness low, they find word-reading and writing highly complicated, and many are soon derailed by the ongoing, complex learning and high cognitive load they experience.

Confused and overwhelmed, lower-third word readers soon start to struggle. Missing out on ongoing success, many develop Acquired Helplessness: inner belief that they're not capable of effectively mastering word-reading and spelling.

Aged only 4.5 to 5 years, many kids pragmatically check out, inwardly deciding to take their bat and ball and go home, with an attitude of *I don't do reading, but it will be over soon, and lunchtime will be fun*. Alas, while the kids aren't concentrating, they miss key learning, and over time their word-reading delay evolves into severe literacy struggles.

Acquired Helplessness has ongoing, sad, negative impacts that slow learning progress. Notably, it makes effective catch-up intervention much more difficult to achieve in our older, crushed and crumpled, cute koalas with entrenched difficulties. Indeed, Acquired Helplessness is likely a major factor impeding the rescuing of our kids with ongoing major word-reading and writing difficulties.

Give Children What They Need

Give Children What They Need refers to the value of knowing each child's instructional needs, then tailoring instruction effectively, so that time isn't wasted, practising skills where instruction isn't needed.

Our CQU research team worked with teachers and schools in one Queensland region from 2013 to 2017 in the *Bridging the Gap* research project, to establish principles of effective instruction for at-risk readers in our early years.

It was a great project, and we loved learning from each other. As part of that learning, we arrived at useful new vocabulary, including

- *Successful Engaged Learning*: Children needing to be both actively engaged in learning, plus achieving ample success in that learning, for it to be effective.
- The *Find the Learning Time Challenge*: Australian schools being immensely time-poor relative to regular-orthography nations, with thus major needs to be strategic in achieving effective learning time.
- *Give Children What They Need*: Tailoring instruction effectively so that time is used valuably, with children receiving the tailored instruction they need.

Giving children what they need in teaching and learning, using assessments and instruction strategically, can save time in many ways. Using word-reading as an example,

- Lower-third word-readers need and would be given hefty emotional supports in addition to academic supports, with lots of systematic instruction and practice building their word-reading skills.
- Robust-progress upper-third readers would have quite minimal explicit instruction on word-reading skills, with most time spent on stimulating, meaning-based reading and activities that are often child-managed.

In addition, all kids would engage in extensive literacy enrichment – which, of course, is easier said than done in our too busy schools. Nonetheless, into the future, it's vital we achieve education that is rich, stimulating and engaging for all three thirds of our kids.

Clearly, the goal is strong effective improvement. We know that very well. Alas, achieving it in our schools at the current time is immensely challenging. Meeting our ever-present Find the Learning Time Challenge, emphasising Successful Engaged Learning, and giving kids the teaching they need, are powerful ways forward, particularly if used within 10 Changes improvements.

The *Bridging the Gap* project report is available online, on ResearchGate. It includes separate lists of instructional principles for reading comprehension, word-reading, and language skills for literacy. They are useful, practical principles towards optimising instruction and intervention.

With instructional principles for upper and lower-third readers differing more in extent of application rather than being different principles per se, the *Bridging the Gap* principles are useful for all three thirds of readers. Towards meeting the needs of at-risk and struggling readers, the report includes a section specifying strategic principles for progressing at-risk and struggling readers.

Change 4: Respect Learning Differences

Change 4 is *One-size education does not fit all: Teach to the decidedly different instructional needs of upper-third and lower-third readers.* It emphasises the tailored instruction that our cute koala kids very much need, particularly while we're using solely Standard English, and have such widely-varying word-reading and writing levels.

Knowledge-building on this area is much needed and will strongly support our progress in optimising education.

Let's research our kids' information processing skills – their cognitive-processing, executive-function, phonological and orthographic awareness, and statistical-learning skills – at the same time as we're researching their literacy and language-skill development.

Let's also add a few useful terms to our vernacular, including *orthographic complexity, working memory, cognitive load, cognitive processing, executive-function skills, statistical learning* and *self-teaching.*

And let's establish the dimensions of those pivotal instructional differences between our thirds.

Change 5
Investigate Word-Reading

It seems likely that it is the high cognitive load of learning to read English that is the crux of both English word-reading development and its role as a gateway skill separating those who succeed in sophisticated literacy from those who do not.

Susan Galletly & Bruce Knight[xxix], 2011

And when my Grade 3 teacher asked me to read out loud, I knew it was going to be another of the worst days of my life.

Richard Branson[xxx]

Change 5 states, *End our data deficiency: Build strong knowledge on word-reading levels.* Let's do that. Let's get knowledgeable about word-reading levels in Australia.

What's Word-Reading?

Word-reading is the ability to read words and word-parts, such as letters and syllables. It includes reading the words kids read in meaningful texts, e.g., in textbooks, books for pleasure and online information. It also includes reading isolated words, e.g., words in lists.

Word-reading development supports development of other literacy skills, including spelling, vocabulary and language skills, reading comprehension and written expression.

In word-reading, kids develop two needed partner skills:
- A growing bank of *sightwords*, words they recognise instantly, on sight.
- Skill for reading unfamiliar words they need to decode, using word-reading skills and strategies.

In regular-orthography nations, virtually all words are regular, and kids thus use a single strategy, *sounding-out*, for reading and writing both familiar and unfamiliar words.

Sounding-out is also at times called *phonemic recoding, decoding,* and the *Alphabetic Principle.* Using letter-sounds and phonemic awareness, kids move back and forward between written and spoken words: recoding from written words to spoken words when reading, and from spoken words to written words when writing.

Interestingly, brain-scan research shows that even when regular-orthography readers read highly-familiar words, the phonemic-recoding path is used. We expert adult Standard English word-readers use that path too.

Because of English orthographic complexity, we have three orthographic grainsizes that match to our three main types of words and syllables: we can call them *Regular, Pattern* and *Tricky* words and syllables. When reading and writing less-familiar words and syllables, kids use three word-reading strategies, matched to the three syllable types:
- They sound-out Regular words and syllables, e.g., *bus, cat, ye̲s̲terday*.
- They use rhyme and common patterns to read Pattern words and syllables, e.g., *-all, -ar, -oy, -ow, yester da̲y̲* – knowing *ball* and *look*, they can read and write *wall, call, small* and *cook, shook, chook.*
- They remember highly-irregular Tricky words and syllables, e.g., *one, two, was, yest e̲r̲day*, visually, by what they look like, remembering their idiosyncrasies, and seek help for unknown words.

Standard English vowel GPCs are our cute koala joeys' biggest challenge. Our myriad of spellings for our 20 common vowel-sounds causes great confusion, particularly when kids lack metacognition and think we've only five vowel-sounds: the common sounds of our five vowel letters.

They're empowered by activities building awareness of how the word *vowel* can mean, at different times,
- Our five commonest vowel-sounds, in *at, egg, it, off, up*.
- Our five vowel letters.
- Our 20 common vowel-sounds.
- Vowel sounds of words and syllables, e.g., b<u>oa</u>t, b<u>e</u>g<u>i</u>n.
- The vowel graphemes in those words and syllables.

The Research Tours explores interesting studies showing reading unfamiliar words to be a pivotal issue for Standard English readers: our nemesis, really, impeding both our weak word-readers and healthy-progress kids.

Word-Reading Is Important

Standard English word-reading is a gateway skill in literacy and life, at both national and international levels.

It separates our struggling word-readers from successful readers, e.g., kids' word-reading levels in Year 1 strongly predict how well they'll achieve in later school years.

Internationally, it's our Standard English word-reading levels that separate us from regular-orthography nations, and their thriving education, and create the many woes of our severe orthographic disadvantage.

Word-reading creates the crosslinguistic divide between the world's many regular-orthography nations, with their speed and ease of word-reading and early-literacy development, and struggling Anglophone nations, Australia included, where 4.5 to 5-year-olds endeavour to read and write Standard English, and many fail to thrive.

In very many ways, word-reading is an important literacy skill, particularly while we use solely Standard English.

It's Time to Start Testing Word-Reading

It's quite astonishing how little data Australian education has on our kids' word-reading levels. It's Swiss-cheese, for sure, and bunyips galore.

Every year, NAPLAN testing of our Year 3, 5, 7 and 9 kids provides national, State and school data on kids' reading comprehension, written expression, spelling, grammar and punctuation – but not word-reading.

In consequence, many lower-third word-readers miss out on the word-reading instruction and intervention they need.

A further sad outcome is our NAPLAN test developers assuming all our kids have sufficient word-reading skills for NAPLAN test items, when this is not the case. Test norms suggest about a third of our Year 3 kids, and up to 20% of Year 5, 7 and 9 kids have insufficient word-reading, and would benefit from test items being read aloud.

Teachers have always known this and so have the parents of our struggling readers. Not having word-reading data has sad impacts on many crushed and crumpled koalas.

Now some might say the reason word-reading isn't tested is because word-reading is usually tested one-to-one, with an adult listening as the child reads, whereas whole-class tests work well for other literacy skills.

Given how important word-reading is, that argument holds little water. That's particularly so, given that word-reading can be tested extremely quickly and efficiently.

Done one-on-one with an adult testing each child, using, e.g., the two subtests of the *Test of Word Reading Efficiency-2* (TOWRE-2), word-reading testing can take less than 5 minutes per child. It could also easily become part of online testing.

If we're to achieve improvement of literacy development and education generally, we must end our current data dearth, and change so we've useful levels of word-reading data at school and national level.

We need strong knowledge on
- Our kids' word-reading levels.
- How their word-reading levels build over time.
- How their word-reading levels relate to development of other literacy and learning skills.
- How word-reading development and instructional needs differ for upper and lower-third word-readers.

We also want to establish how effectively our schools can routinely teach and remediate our lower-third and lowest-tenth word-readers, so that they too proficiently master word-reading and spelling.

Further, we want to know ease, speed and time-duration aspects of word-reading and spelling development, and how our kids compare with regular-orthography kids, for thirds, tenths, and our highest and lowest 5% and 2% of achievers.

Understanding these aspects of word-reading development is an essential part of our knowledge-building towards improving our cute koalas' literacy and learning skill development, and Australian education generally.

It's therefore time for change, to routinely assessing word-reading across primary and high school. Initially, there'd be value in assessing word-reading in our TAFEs and universities as well.

While it's not something we've done routinely to date, testing word-reading is a change we need to accept and work with.

So let's assess word-reading and monitor our cute koalas' word-reading development.

Word-Reading Data for School Instruction

Our schools need word-reading data to support their tailoring of reading instruction to kids' instructional needs.

At present, Australian education emphasises Capital-R Reading, Reading Comprehension, and its instruction, with relatively little emphasis on small-r reading, word-reading, and its instruction.

This does a major disservice to our struggling word-readers who need tailored word-reading instruction. Word-reading studies conducted across Years 1 to 8 by our CQU team suggest at least 30% of kids have significantly weak word-reading by Anglosphere standards. Of course, by regular-orthography standards, both our middle and lower-third word-readers are dreadfully delayed, and even most of our upper-third kids are well behind.

School reading data tends to mirror our educational climate of strong emphasis on reading comprehension (Capital-R Reading), and relatively little emphasis on word-reading (small-r reading). Most schools thus have copious data on their kids' reading-comprehension levels, but little-to-no data on word-reading levels, except in the first year or so.

Not surprisingly, given this sad lack of word-reading data, school reading instruction often focuses almost completely on building reading comprehension with very little focus on building word-reading, from Year 2 on.

With our kids' word-reading taking so long to develop, at least six years, on average, to reach a reasonable level, our omitting focus on word-reading across primary-school years is disappointing and inappropriate.

We teach and test spelling and reading comprehension across primary and high school, but we leave teaching and testing of spelling's partner skill, word-reading, to just the first school years. That's a highly illogical bunyip.

A further bunyip is how the Reading Wars arguments our journalists enthusiastically report on, are rarely based on Aussie facts and data – because we don't have facts and data to be discussed – because we don't test word-reading and monitor word-reading development. Another bunyip.

We ignore word-reading at our peril as, doubtless, our not knowing our word-reading levels adds to our education woes.

Knowing kids' word-reading levels will empower schools' literacy instruction easily as much as it will empower national knowledge-building.

It may also empower our national curriculum. Given we've a wide range of word-reading levels in most classrooms, and many weak word-readers in all school years, our schools need ample resources for word-reading instruction and intervention. Our schools need well resourced, integrated teaching of word-reading, vocabulary and spelling, as Japan and Taiwan do, with resources provided at national level.

Word-reading would also be part of that streamlined Australian Curriculum strand we need for our struggling readers, which strategically increases time to build needed literacy and numeracy basics, through use of tailored options that reduce literacy demands in subject-area learning.

When teachers and schools know students' current word-reading levels, they can tailor instruction to their specific needs far more effectively. Without that data, they can't.

Giving kids what they need, using word-reading data, our literacy instruction for stronger-progress word-readers would be largely meaning-based, building language, thinking and literacy skills, and including the small amount of systematic word-reading instruction they need, which empowers their self-teaching and progress.

Again giving kids what they need, for kids with weaker word-reading skills, literacy instruction would include appropriate, systematic, tailored word-reading instruction. We can't do that at present. Data is needed.

With our struggling readers having high workload, it's pivotal we don't waste learning time, and strategically focus instruction on the areas where kids need it.

Our three main groups of struggling readers with reading-comprehension weakness have specific subskill patterns:
- Weakness in both language skills and word-reading.
- Healthy language skills, but weak word-reading.
- Healthy word-reading, but weak language skills.

We need Australian research on those three groups. It's Swiss-cheese time currently, regarding Aussie numbers in each group, as we've only reading-comprehension data.

The Research Tours explores USA research that suggests
- Word-reading difficulties are the major issue for most struggling readers in the early years of schooling.
- Word-reading and language weakness occur with similar frequency in older struggling readers.
- Considerable numbers in all years have weakness in both word-reading and language skills.

When schools don't have word-reading data, their weak word-readers often don't receive needed word-reading instruction, and instead receive reading-comprehension instruction, whose effectiveness is reduced because of the kids' weak word-reading. We need to change that.

Useful Word-Reading Tests

Until and unless we develop our own Australian word-reading efficiency tests, I recommend we use the *Test of Word Reading Efficiency-2* (TOWRE-2) and word-reading tests discussed below. They provide strategic information while taking little time to administer and score.

The Test of Word Reading Efficiency-2 (TOWRE-2)

The TOWRE-2 is a rigorous, quick-to-use word-reading efficiency test, which involves reading two word-lists, each for 45 seconds.

Efficiency tests measure the number of words kids read correctly in a set short period of time. They're much quicker to use than untimed tests, which some struggling readers read laboriously. They're also kind to struggling readers, as with the time period quite short, kids don't experience obvious, lengthy struggles.

The TOWRE-2's two easily-scored subtests assess word-reading's two partner skills, sightwords and reading of unfamiliar words. The *Sight Word Efficiency* subtest tests sightword reading, using a list of highly-familiar words of increasing length and complexity. The *Phonemic Decoding Efficiency* subtest assesses reading of unfamiliar words, similarly using words of increasing length and complexity.

We need our Federal Government to provide every primary school, high school and TAFE with the TOWRE-2. We should also save trees, and avoid its paper record forms that we'd drown in, instead using digital record-keeping.

The TOWRE is quick to administer and easily scored, plus it's normed from age six to 25 years, so can be used across primary and high school. Having four parallel versions, it can also be easily used for retesting over time, e.g., in annual skill monitoring, or to assess progress made from a period of intensive intervention.

Our CQU research team and regional schools have used the TOWRE extensively in collaborative research studies. Almost invariably, teachers love it for its time-saving efficiency and powerful data, with many schools then using it routinely in their monitoring of reading development.

The TOWRE-2, or similar tests Aussies develop, would be very powerful to use in NAPLAN, testing reading of both sightwords and unfamiliar words, perhaps initially in a 10% sample of our Year 3, 5, 7 and 9 kids doing NAPLAN.

We could also easily add testing with the TOWRE-2 for all our kids engaging in PIRLS and PISA studies.

Useful Diagnostic Word-Reading Tests

In addition to kids' word-reading levels, our schools need diagnostic information that guides instruction usefully and specifically.

While the TOWRE-2 quickly and efficiently provides powerful information on kids' word-reading levels, it's less powerful in providing diagnostic information, e.g., quickly showing the specific types of words where weakness exists.

Other word-reading tests, which are equally quick to administer, can usefully provide this diagnostic data.

There's value in schools using these assessments in their skill monitoring. That way, schools might monitor how quickly and thoroughly children master particular sets of words, e.g., irregular words, and those with specific vowel (V) and consonant (C) combinations, such as the following:

- Regular CVC, CVCe and CCVCC words, e.g., *hat, hate, grant.*
- Unfamiliar CVC, CVCe and CCVCC words, e.g., *zat, zate, brant.*
- Irregular words in our 200 most-frequent words.
- Regular words using common two-letter vowels, e.g., w*ai*t, fl*oa*t, ch*ar*t, str*ay*, sp*oi*l, and unfamiliar words with these patterns, e.g., z*ai*t, br*oa*t, sp*ar*t, sn*ay*, str*oi*l.
- Two-syllable, somewhat-regular words, e.g., *supper/super, hopping/hoping*, and unfamiliar words with the same patterns, e.g., *zupper/zuper, zopping/zoping.*
- Longer, less-frequent, easily-confused words, e.g., addition, addiction, aptitude, altitude, attitude, attitudinal, and unfamiliar words, e.g., annition, anniction, antitude, amtitude, abtitude, abtitudinal.
- Irregular words in our 200 to 10,000 most frequent words of English.

As you'll see from convincing findings of key studies *The Research Tours* explores, it's powerful to assess kids' skills on specific word groups, as this spotlights the particular word-reading areas where they need instruction.

Some free tests that I've developed, which are available on ResearchGate, might be useful for this purpose, e.g., the *Galletly Diagnostic Vowel Word Reading Tests*, which are brief 30 second tests, and *Galletly 50-Word Probes*, which test reading of our 200 most frequent words, using random samples that include approximately every fourth word.

It would be easy to develop school, regional and national norms for tests such as these. Using the tests with large numbers of children in different year-levels, along with a standardised test such as the TOWRE-2, enables norms to then be calculated.

If a group of schools worked collaboratively with university researchers, using the tests and collating their data, they'd develop useful year-level norms, with percentile levels and cut-offs, for identifying kids at-risk or needing intervention.

We could also develop other quick-to-use tests, e.g., tests of multisyllabic-word groups, and 50 or 100 word samples for reading the 500, 1,000, 5,000 and 10,000 most-frequent words that kids encounter in reading.

Let's Measure Automisation Weakness

Automisation weakness, difficulty mastering skills without them slipping and later being forgotten, is common in our lower-third and lowest-tenth word-readers: kids forget key skills that seemed mastered, but alas weren't automatic.

Automisation weakness commonly impacts the word groups listed above, and also counting-down by numbers and learning number-facts, such as the 2-times-tables.

Automisation weakness is a sad bunyip that adds sizeable teaching and learning workload. Forgotten skills not only need reteaching, but can also hide if they're not monitored, and then impede next steps of learning in nasty ways.

In two of my books that build word-reading, *Sounds & Vowels* and *Two Vowels Talking*, memory-stretching grids are included for key skills where kids often lose progress without teachers or family noticing. Kids' skill levels can be recorded on the grids over time, which quickly reveals when levels have slipped and need renewed focus.

I include memory stretching because it's so common for our struggling word-readers to not retain, and then lose, word-reading skills that aren't automatic, when those skills are no longer being practised.

We'd benefit by research exploring automisation weakness and its sad impacts, including how it reduces teaching and learning efficiency, and adds to child and teacher workload.

Let's Save Time When Testing

Of our schools that do assess word-reading across the primary-school years, many use lengthy one-on-one tests that test both word-reading and reading comprehension.

These, alas, can consume considerable learning time, as teachers assess each child one by one.

Time spent testing is time not spent teaching, thus we benefit when testing of word-reading takes minimal time for ample gain. Importantly, separating testing of reading comprehension and language comprehension from testing of word-reading enables much saving of time.

Whole-class or small-group testing can be used quite easily for reading comprehension and language comprehension. Then, time-saving, quick, efficiency tests such as TOWRE-2 can be used for the one-to-one testing of word-reading.

Importantly, with speech-to-text software now working increasingly well in digital applications, we need to explore computerised word-reading testing with the TOWRE-2 and other efficient word-reading tests, e.g., tests of the word groups discussed above.

Let's Do Minimal Testing of Our Upper-Third

It's not just in literacy development that our upper and lower-thirds differ. They also differ in the extent to which skills need to be assessed. That's definitely the case for word-reading, and cognitive-processing skills that underlie effective word-reading.

After initial knowledge-building, it's likely word-reading testing of upper-third word-readers would be minimal.

Key cognitive-processing skills and word-reading readiness might be assessed in the early years, establishing kids' areas of strength. Occasional monitoring would then still be useful over the years, as some kids develop word-reading difficulties for unfamiliar words beyond the early years.

Perhaps annual testing using the TOWRE-2 subtests might be used, administered by trained teacher-aides, or using digital testing. Another option would be to test word-reading in online Year 3, 5, 7 and 9 NAPLAN testing.

In contrast, for children with weaker word-reading skills, more frequent, quick, efficient testing would be the order of the day, with the test data that's gathered then used to guide the instruction and intervention that kids receive.

Let's Do School-Level Research

Australian education would benefit greatly by strategic school-level research on word-reading and literacy skills.

Here are 10 useful areas well-worth exploring, with potential to quickly build key knowledge we need:

1. Our kids' word-reading levels across year-levels.
2. Relationships between kids' cognitive-processing, word-reading, spelling, language-skill and reading-comprehension skills across year-levels.
3. How different methods for building word-reading impact word-reading development.
4. Differences between upper and lower-third word-readers in responsiveness to those methods.
5. How cognitive processing, phonological awareness, statistical learning and self-teaching impact word-reading, spelling and early-literacy development.
6. Differences in resourcing needed to achieve effective word-reading and spelling development, in upper, middle and lower-third word-readers.
7. Developing Australian norms for currently used word-reading tests, including the TOWRE-2, and diagnostic word-reading tests.
8. Comparing word-reading development of the full range of word-readers, in Australia and other nations, focusing on
   a. The extent of resourcing and time needed to reach confident, accurate self-teaching, then high accuracy, then high fluency.
   b. Learning hours needed for word-reading and spelling development.
   c. Characteristics and effectiveness of different word-reading instruction methods.
9. Exploring how to optimise Standard-English word-reading intervention, and the resourcing needed.
10. Exploring the impact of potentially useful change mechanisms, including
    a. Fully-regular beginners' orthographies.
    b. Older starting ages.
    c. Greater readiness building.

We'll find this knowledge-building useful and informative.

The Challenge of Lowest-Tenth Word-Readers

There's every likelihood that sometime in the future, we'll have Australian decision-making on whether to adopt an initial, fully-regular beginners' orthography, or continue with Standard English without a beginners' orthography.

Two key reasons for changing will be easing and speeding literacy development for all our cute koalas, and reducing the expense of early-years education and intervention.

A third key reason will be the extreme difficulty we have achieving effective word-reading development in our lowest-tenth word readers, and the massive resourcing we'll need, if we're to support them through to strong progress, and ongoing success in reading and writing.

These will be pivotal factors in our decision-making.

Word-reading instruction is especially challenging for the weakest 5 to 10% of word-readers. That's five to 10 kids in each hundred – one to three kids in each class of 25.

These weakest word-readers usually need ongoing, expert, systematic, one-on-one and small-group instruction, if they are to make steady progress.

Then, even with intensive intervention, they often continue to struggle, with word-reading and spelling levels years below their classmates.

As studies in *The Research Tours* explore, most progress somewhat, but don't move up to healthy word-reading and spelling, and stay there – and they're woefully far from the levels that regular-orthography lowest-tenth kids achieve.

One small subgroup of intelligent cute koala kids, perhaps our weakest 2% of word-readers, make extremely slow progress despite very extensive expert intervention. In research studies, they're sometimes termed *treatment resisters* or *nonresponders*.

Bunyips, anyone?

These crushed and crumpled koala kids usually have extremely weak cognitive-processing skills, and a family history of significant word-reading or spelling difficulties.

We need Australian research exploring the extent to which schools can routinely achieve optimal Standard English word-reading development in our weakest 2%, 5% and 10% of word-readers, comparing them with regular-orthography kids. This information is much needed.

We may find that appropriate resourcing and instruction combined with later starting age results in lowest-tenth word-readers achieving healthy word-reading development.

Equally, we may find Standard English without use of a beginners' orthography is simply too expensive to continue, because of the massive extent of resourcing that schools would need to achieve healthy word-reading in our lowest-tenth word-readers.

Further, we may also find that our schools can't routinely achieve healthy word-reading and spelling in these at-risk kids, even with optimal intervention and resourcing.

How well we can achieve for our lowest-tenth word-readers and writers will be pivotal in decisions we make, as regards 10 Changes improvements.

We'll likely find the minimal progress rates our Standard English lowest-tenth make, along with the resourcing needed, to be immensely sobering, when we compare it with regular-orthography progress and resourcing.

That sad cost-benefit ratio may well swing our decision-making over to us first using a fully-regular beginners' orthography, before Standard English.

Importantly, in all our word-reading and spelling research, we'll need to consider how time is spent and saved:
- Spent, on word-reading instruction and remediation, and supporting struggling readers, when we use just Standard English.

- Saved, through both learning time and word-reading and spelling difficulties being minimal, when we use a fully-regular beginners' orthography.

Change 5: Investigate Word-reading

Change 5 states, *End our data deficiency: Build strong knowledge on word-reading levels.*

Let's investigate word-reading. It's much needed.

As part of that, let's assess our kids' word-reading skills, and monitor their word-reading development over time, using quick, easy-to-use tests that generate useful data and information for guiding both teaching and learning in schools, and national decision-making.

This information will help us explore the relationship of word-reading to other literacy skills and subskills. It will also allow us to compare our kids' word-reading with that of other nations.

This is knowledge-building we crucially need. It will play a key role in our improving of literacy development and education generally.

Change 6
Enrich Education for Every Child

The mind is not a vessel to be filled, but a fire to be kindled.

Plutarch[xxxi]

An understanding heart is everything in a teacher ... One looks back with appreciation to the brilliant teachers, but with gratitude to those who touched our human feelings. The curriculum is so much necessary raw material, but warmth is the vital element for the growing plant and for the soul of the child.

Carl Jung[xxxii]

Change 6 is emphatic: *Enrich every child: Ensure effective, supportive, tailored education.*

Let's do that. Let's not over-focus on lower or upper-third kids, and instead focus on the preciousness and needs of each and every child.

As part of that, let's know kids' levels on important literacy skills, and provide expert tailored teaching.

Enrichment includes strong focus on language skills. While Change 5 focused on word-reading and its assessment, our kids' language skills are a major focus of Change 6.

Every one of our cute koalas has major needs for skilfully differentiated teaching that expedites vigorous literacy and learning development.

They also have major needs for mentoring – comfortably chatting with teachers, confident that at least one school adult understands them well and considers them extremely important, providing wise encouraging words that nurture them along their learning and life journey.

In meeting both kids' academic and social-emotional needs, we'll make a huge difference – for each cute koala kid, for Australia, and towards improving Australian education.

At the current time it's likely we're providing insufficiently-enriched and insufficiently-supportive education for all three thirds of our kids. Our 15-year-olds said that loud and clear in PISA 2018, about our unruly classrooms – how they're finding school life immensely frustrating, so much so that they positioned us as eighth worst in the world as regards classroom climate being conducive to learning.

Talking with teachers, teacher aides and parents endlessly relays the same story.

Our teachers and teacher aides would love to have the time they need to get alongside each cute koala kid and chat while supporting learning, showing understanding of, and interest in, the child's world. But there's too little time to do this consistently at present, as covering the required curriculum is, in itself, a major time struggle.

In addition, teachers report that considerably more kids seem anxious: stressed because teaching and learning is too often rushed. Many kids feel continually behind, chasing their tails, not sufficiently on top of learning, and far from being confidently in control.

Parents discuss their children's struggles, and there too, frustration and struggles seem the norm for all three thirds, a long way from optimal, enriched education.

Parents of advanced-progress, upper-third students discuss their kids being too much ignored, and too often left to work on their own. Our parents also comment on boredom and disengagement being increasingly an issue for these kids.

Parents of average-progress, middle-third students discuss the curriculum moving too quickly in primary school and there being too many complex assignments in high school, such that kids feel somewhat overwhelmed and disengaged.

Parents of struggling lower-third students feel sad: they're disappointed that the rich education they'd thought their kids would receive has been so depressingly inadequate.

Their kids are sad too. In addition, naïvely trusting that it can't be our system that's at fault, they all too often blame themselves for their difficulties, taking their frustrations inward, building anxiety and depression.

School life is also far too busy and pressured – it's just not fun! One insightful child I worked with summed up the current situation well. School used to be rainbows, but now it's just plain grey. We need to bring that rich colour back, leaving HEARTSH behind and seizing GENTLE.

Relatively few cute koalas get the well-resourced and well-supported education our Education Act promises.

Fortunately, comprehensive education for every child is the law here. So let's get to work and achieve it, using 10 Changes improvements. Let's ensure we meet our teaching challenges, and achieve effective education that's vastly more enriched for every cute koala kid.

Let's Focus on both Language Enrichment and Personal Enrichment

In enriching our children's education, let's focus on enriching language and thinking. Let's also focus on personal enrichment.

Change 6 prioritises time for effective enrichment, and time is currently a challenge. Fortunately, our using a beginners' orthography, after we've actioned Change 8, will provide ample time for enrichment and learning purposes.

Change 6's enriching of education also overlaps Change 9: *First, play to learn: Start Standard English word-reading instruction from mid-Year 2*. Together, Changes 8 and 9 will enable strong enrichment through our kids so quickly and easily developing confident reading and writing, and us then being time-rich: saving the mega-hours we currently spend developing word-reading and spelling, and supporting our seriously struggling readers.

Let's focus firmly on our cute koalas' needs for language enrichment. Language skills are central to kids' literacy, learning and life development. In fact, they're crucially important. As part of that we'll monitor kids' language skill development, perhaps initially through that 10% NAPLAN sample I'm suggesting.

We'd assess kids' language reasoning, inferencing and comprehension. We'd also assess expressive and receptive vocabulary. In expressive vocabulary, kids are shown pictures they name, e.g., of a cot, helicopter, igloo, and microphone. In receptive vocabulary, they're told a word, e.g., *liquid*, then select which one of a group of pictures best represents that concept.

Receptive and expressive vocabulary are separate skills in key ways. Our kids with Language, Literacy and Learning Disorder (LLLD), i.e., Developmental Language Disorder and Dyslexia, often have healthy receptive vocabulary, but struggle badly with expressive vocabulary, due to cognitive-processing weakness and associated word-finding struggles. They have difficulty efficiently retrieving the words they want to use from long-term memory, and often say an incorrect term instead, e.g., saying *train/bus, read/write*.

In the future, when Australia is firmly focused on language-skills enrichment, it's likely schools will routinely monitor language-skills development.

As with word-reading, this will involve decidedly less testing for cute koalas with strong language skills, and more frequent and more detailed testing of kids who have weak language skills.

Let's also focus firmly on personal enrichment, including mentoring and personal development.

Our Find the Caring Time Challenge really is as serious as our Find the Learning Time Challenge. Both teachers and teacher aides so often comment on our children needing both encouragement and the relaxed chatting that happens easily in confident relationships, and how they so regret that there's not the time for this to happen.

Into the future, we'd ensure an effective focus on mentoring and personal development, particularly for more vulnerable cute koalas. We need our kids increasingly confident, with healthy self-esteem and self-management skills.

We might combine this with teachers having the same class for two to three years as many European nations do. Our Aussie habit of our teachers changing classes every year reduces our potential for achieving the effective mentoring and supportive trust-filled relationships that our kids need.

Yes, let's ensure enrichment of language and thinking skills, and personal development.

Finland's and Estonia's GENTLE Seems Worthy

I love sitting in and watching education in Finnish and Estonian schools. They very impressively achieve Gentle, Engaging, Never-Tiring, Learning Enrichment (GENTLE).

I love their emphasis on kids not being overworked, and how they prioritise music, physical activity and breaks, so education is well-balanced.

I love their 15-minute break after each lesson, so kids get a chance to reflect, move, chat and have fun, and teachers aren't pressured to rush into their next lesson, and chat casually with and mentor kids.

I love the time that Finnish and Estonian schools gain by primary-school subject-area testing being so minimal, and how they're aghast at the amount of in-class testing and report-card writing that we do across primary school.

I love how teachers and allied-health staff have sufficient time to meet together to discuss kids' needs, and to provide timely small-group and one-on-one support.

I love how initially I smiled at how they seemed to coddle their 7 and 8-year-olds, in the extensive supports and gentle kindness they provide. Then, reflecting, I realised I was WYSYAINing, with my amusement not appropriate.

Their attitudes and actions are appropriate, supportive and compassionate, while we're being far too tough. Doubtless, we exacerbate our education woes through insisting our littlies work so long and hard, when so young.

I also love how their Special Education is for all kids, not just struggling learners, and how it's far from the life sentence it can be here. Their kids of all thirds move in and out of Special Education, accessing remedial or enrichment support for the time it's needed.

Of course, Finland and Estonia can do this far more easily than we can, as they've strong orthographic advantage.

Our budgets would blow out irreparably if we implemented GENTLE and its practices here now, with 4.5 and 5-year-olds learning to read and write solely Standard English.

In addition, GENTLE wouldn't work effectively while we're using Standard English without a beginners' orthography, and starting kids so young on learning to read and write. We'd spend excessively for insufficient gains.

We first need 10 Changes improvements that give us rapid, easy, highly effective early-literacy development, along with ample time and far fewer struggling learners. These set the scene for nations to easily achieve GENTLE.

Finland and Estonia are both regular-orthography nations, so they don't have our time-pressure. They enjoy their Es, a.k.a. Ease, being Easy Education Nations that optimise their orthographic advantage. They have Easy, Expedited, Efficient, Effective Education that's delightfully Effortless.

It contrasts markedly with our struggles. After all, we're yet to become a Semi-Easy Education Nation with a beginners' orthography, enjoying Es and Ease, and the Easy, Expedited Efficient, Effective Education that we'd so love to have here.

We're currently stuck in our mire of Cs:
- We're a Chaotic, Cluttered-Curriculum Nation.
- Our kids experience Confused, Complex learning and too high Cognitive load.
- Our schools wrestle with our Confused, Chaotic, Complicated, Cluttered-Curriculum Conundrum of having to spend too much time developing fledgling literacy skills, and thus having too little time for the many other important areas of education.

We need to leave Cs behind and take up Es instead. We can do that, quite easily, using 10 Changes improvements.

To a certain extent, where we'd like to move to and where we are now, are a contrast of GENTLE and HEARTSH.

We're currently stuck in HEARTSH, with school life often being that frustrating Hugely-Exhausting, Actually-Rather-Tedious Schooling Heaviness. We've had far too much of HEARTSH lately, dull grey instead of rich colours.

We'd love to move to GENTLE, and an education system and climate that incorporates Gentle, Engaging, Never-Tiring, Learning Enrichment easily and well.

Let's prioritise GENTLE, positioning it as a key goal in our improving of education here.

Let's Leave HEARTSH Behind.

I've used the acronym HEARTSH rather than HARSH (*Harsh AnxiousCed Schooling Heaviness*), to promote thinking on heart aspects of education.

Let's move education here away from our current somewhat hard-hearted and cold-hearted education. Let's instead take on education that's soft-hearted, kind-hearted, and warm-hearted, and uses highly child-focused teaching and learning that kids, teachers and families all love.

Yes, as part of improving education, let's end HEARTSH.

Parents, wouldn't you love it if the instruction each of your kids received was nicely tailored, matched to your child's individual strengths, weaknesses, needs and interests?

Our teachers and allied-health providers would love it too.

It's not acceptable that our kids spend 300 hours more in school each year than kids in other nations, and that we're achieving so poorly. It's not acceptable for our kids to be so disengaged and frustrated that our classrooms rank among the most disruptive in the world.

It's not acceptable that our teachers do 200 more class-teaching hours each year than other nations, along with and the preparation and administration each hour entails. It's not acceptable that so many great teachers are leaving the profession, having decided enough is enough.

It's not acceptable that our schools don't have the time they need to provide effective, tailored education and mentoring, which our cute koala kids so desperately need.

Change 6: Enrich Education for Every Child

Change 6 is *Enrich every child: Ensure effective, supportive, tailored education.*

We want all our children to be motivated and extended, known and mentored well, and receive enriched education matched to strengths, weaknesses, needs and interests.

Our Education Act says we should be doing this.

So too does our 2019 Alice Springs (Mparntwe) Education Declaration.

Importantly, so do the UN Convention on the Rights of the Child and UN Convention on the Rights of Persons with Disabilities, to which we're signatory.

So, let's do it!

Let's make the enrichment of every child's education a key priority in our improving of education.

Change 7
Insist on Easier Literacy Development

You never change things by fighting the existing reality. To change something, build a new model that makes the existing model obsolete.

Daniel Quinn[xxxiii]

A problem adequately stated is a problem solved theoretically ...
And therefore subsequently to be solved, realistically.

R Buckminster Fuller[xxxiv]

Change 7 is *Insist on easier early-literacy development: Reach regular-orthography nations' achievement levels.*

That might seem a very big ask now, circa 2022. But just watch things change over time, as we build 10 Changes research knowledge, and action 10 Changes improvements.

Surely our kids ethically have a right to easier, faster word-reading and literacy development.

Why?

Because much easier, very rapid word-reading, writing and early-literacy development is routinely achieved across schools in the world's many regular-orthography nations, with vastly fewer children struggling with word-reading and writing, and their difficulties being quite mild.

Easy Expedited Early Literacy is the Norm

If our situation, of slow, drawn-out word-reading, spelling and early-literacy development, and such large numbers of seriously struggling readers, was the norm in all nations, our status quo would be acceptable.

But that's not the case, and we've been sadly WYSYAINing. That's why we need our ABCs, so we ACT locally while we look globally, BOOST the lower-third to benefit everyone, and CHANGE effectively to work less and achieve more.

The situation is decidedly different, very much so, in the world's many regular-orthography nations. They routinely meet their teaching challenges very effectively, and achieve highly successful education for their kids.

Early-literacy development happens with delightful ease in regular-orthography nations. Likelihood of word-reading and spelling difficulties is minimal, and likelihood of reading-comprehension difficulties is also much reduced.

Regular-orthography nations and their easier education are more the international norm, while the Anglosphere with our too slow Standard English literacy development and education struggles are rather the exception. They're the relaxed majority, and we're the stressed minority. They're wonderfully successful at child, school, education-system and national level; while we continue to struggle badly, amidst our Early Years Factory, sad Spelling Generations and widespread education woes.

The future is bright; we really do need to move there.

And it all starts with us insisting on similarly easy, rapid early-literacy development.

Logically, regular-orthography nations' ease and speed of early-literacy development sets the bar – the standard we must achieve here.

That's why our ethical early-literacy education goal for Australian education is emphatic:

> *By 2035, Australian education will be*
> *routinely, efficiently, gently and easily*
> *achieving highly effective, rapid development of*
> *children's word-reading, spelling, reading, writing*
> *and early-literacy skills,*
> *in GENTLE manner,*
> *in every early-years classroom,*
> *in all schools across our nation,*
> *as efficiently as is achieved routinely*
> *across schools in regular-orthography nations*
> *such as Taiwan, Japan and China,*
> *with at least 98% of Australian school children*
> *being confident, independent readers and writers,*
> *able to read 95% of the 10,000 most-frequent words,*
> *by age 8.5 years, or within 18 months of starting*
> *formal word-reading instruction.*

It's Time to Take Ethical Action

What do you think?

Aren't our kids entitled to similar ease?

It is ethically unacceptable that Aussie kids are hit with such major struggles in learning to read and write, and greatly increased likelihood of literacy difficulties, simply because they were born here, and not Estonia or Taiwan.

Let's insist our kids have early-literacy development that's as gentle and rapid as schools across regular-orthography nations routinely achieve.

We're the so-called Lucky Country, but our current choices make us decidedly unlucky. Fortunately, we can change.

Are we currently being fair to our kids – all our kids, and particularly our crushed and crumpled koalas who struggle so much with literacy and learning?

No, we're not.

Have we been fair to our kids and adults with entrenched ongoing weak literacy skills, our Spelling Generations?

Most definitely not.

Too many of our struggling readers and spellers are victims of English spelling, our unwitting national choices of orthography and age, with us insisting our kids must learn to read and write our extremely complex Standard-English orthography so young without a beginners' orthography.

Our poor joeys, our crushed and crumpled, struggling readers and our teachers are paying the high cost of orthographic disadvantage in ongoing struggles that are utterly undeserved.

In schools I've visited in regular-orthography nations, be they in Wales, South Korea, Taiwan, Italy, Estonia, Japan or Finland, I'm consistently, always, every time, utterly impressed by the ease of kids' word-reading, spelling and literacy development in early-years classes.

In later-years classes, I'm equally impressed with their uninterrupted teaching and learning, which is happening because kids are so highly literate and such confident, independent learners. That's their norm, not just in exceptional schools, but routinely across all schools.

Their kids' blissfully-easy start to education sets them up for a continued, smooth, gentle, education journey across their school years and beyond.

With all their kids reading and writing independently with high accuracy from Grade 2, learning in subject-area lessons is vastly gentler, and it's able to be achieved so much more efficiently and effectively. And child and teacher workloads are nicely manageable, as is time for subject-area learning.

Relative to us, that's definitely Easy Education, as PIRLS and PISA academic and school-satisfaction results clearly show, e.g., regular-orthography nations achieve well, with far fewer low achievers, and kids show strong satisfaction with their school learning environments.

That's the rich education our kids are also entitled to.

It's also the rich education they're currently not receiving.

Our teenagers were voicing immense frustration with our rushed chaos in PISA 2018. Over 40% of our PISA teenagers reported noise and disorder in most or every English lesson. Further, at least 20% reported they couldn't work well in most lessons, that all too often many students don't listen sufficiently to teachers, and that considerable time is lost before classes settle, and teaching can begin.

The problem starts early, from start of school, due to our education systems' choices. There's every likelihood most of our high-school difficulties commence in our Early Years Factory, through our choices of

- Using solely Standard English orthography without a beginners' orthography.
- Our very young starting age for learning to read.
- Insufficient allied-health supports prior to school.
- Insufficient school resourcing and supports.

Our education woes having their basis in our early-years supports and actions almost hints of child neglect, abuse and harassment. Oh dear! More sad bunyips.

Surely our kids have rights for protection, and not to suffer needless frustrations and struggles inflicted on them by our nation's current choices. Equally, they have rights to smooth, easy, expedited early-literacy development as easy as schools achieve across regular-orthography nations.

It's a sociocultural issue – our poor choices that produce our major child and societal stress and struggles.

Fortunately, choices are options, and ones we can change.

Setting the Bar High is Essential

Solving our education woes starts with us setting the bar equitably high for early-literacy development here, then getting to work achieving it.

It's crucial that we set that bar high and insist our kids have equity. Doing so is the difference between continuing our sad status quo and achieving massive improvement.

Let's face it – setting mediocre goals all too easily achieves mediocrity, and to date we've been exceptional at that.

To aim for anything less than equity with nations with regular-orthographies does a huge disservice to our kids and our potential for exponentially improving education. Setting too low goals will keep us on the back foot, and prevent us from achieving the impressive improvement that we're so eminently capable of.

It really is essential that we set the bar equitably high!

So let's set our bar, the standard we must reach, as early-literacy development as easy and effective as that which schools routinely achieve in Taiwan, Japan and China.

They too have highly-complex orthographies, just as we do. They're also powerful role models, in how they've already actioned the changes that we need to, in having introduced fully-regular beginners' orthographies for their kids' early-literacy development.

In doing so, they quickly left behind the struggles of severe orthographic disadvantage, and moved instead into rich orthographic advantage. They've achieved rapid, vigorous, highly effective early-literacy development, as well as robust education and impressive economic growth. We'd like that.

While I've not visited China, I've observed and explored education in both Taiwan and Japan, and I'm confident it would be powerful to work with those nations if they're amenable, developing research partnerships that build the knowledge we need. South Korea, which introduced fully-regular Hanguel, after World War II, to strong effect, is another powerful role model that's close-by.

Let's also set the bar as achieving Finland and Estonia's GENTLE, their enticing Gentle, Engaging, Never-Tiring, Learning Enrichment, and do research with those nations.

It's possible you're feeling that the bar is set far too high.

It's not! Taiwan, Japan, China and Korea have made these changes, and they've worked meteorically well.

They had literacy woes far worse than ours, and far more struggling readers and illiterate adults, before they changed; and now they're outstanding educational and economic success stories. Their impressive educational and economic rise shows the multifaceted improvement that's ready and waiting for us too, if we so choose.

Importantly, Australia has actioned reforms of similar magnitude very effectively in the past. We changed from pounds, shillings and pennies to decimal currency in 1966, and did it simply and well. Continuing change to the metric system, we left behind the inconvenience of gallons, ounces and inches in the 1970s, with much excitement and little difficulty.

Those are changes other Anglophone nations quite likely envy, but haven't yet achieved.

We were impressive in the changes we took on then. And we can be equally impressive in the logical, sensible, practical education changes we take on in the future.

Setting the bar appropriately high is not just sensible – it's a step we desperately need to take if we're to make the meteoric improvement we're well capable of, and which our kids deserve, and are entitled to.

The Options We'll Explore

One of the reasons I've arrived at the 10 Changes, key directions for Australia to explore and action, is because it's not a simple matter for us to set the bar that high.

However, it's essential that we do so.

Yes, we've lots of work to get on with, to achieve literacy development as smooth and efficient as Taiwan, Japan and China achieve, and Finland's and Estonia's GENTLE.

Working harder at what we currently do is not the answer. When we do what we've always done, we'll get what we've always got – the struggling literacy and education woes we need to leave far behind.

To change and move forward effectively, we need to quickly and strategically do the 10 Changes knowledge-building we require, and then set action plans in place.

That will enable us to move education improvement from Titanic-style to racing-yacht speed and efficiency. We too will be a success story, with our kids too riding Bullet and Express trains to literacy and learning success.

I'm not prescribing the action paths that we'll take to achieve our 2035 goal.

I am suggesting sensible directions for knowledge-building.

Possible directions we'll need to explore will likely include
1. Optimising of Standard English word-reading and spelling development, by providing schools with the resourcing they'll need to explore achieving effective word-reading and spelling development.
2. Trialling using a fully-regular English beginners' orthography initially, then transitioning to Standard English when kids have confident early literacy and learning skills, just as our role models, Taiwan, Japan and China have done.
3. Comparing the effectiveness of, and the resourcing required for, the above options: optimising Standard English instruction vs initially using a beginners' orthography, prior to Standard English.
4. Providing in the pre-school years the allied-health intervention supports that at-risk children need for optimised early-childhood development: by reducing risk factors, readying kids for learning to read and write, and supporting them as needed.
5. Exploring starting formal word-reading instruction at the age many European regular-orthography nations do, at 7 to 8 years, with our first 2.5 years being play-based language and learning enrichment.
6. Using state-of-the-art classroom technology across our schools, including speech-to-text software for writing, and text-to-speech scanners for reading.
7. Providing appropriate supports to class teachers, as leading nations do, including less teaching hours, full-

time teacher aides, improved learning supports, and improved Australian Curriculum resourcing.
8. Providing appropriate supports for our struggling readers, including, for every 500 enrolled children, a learning-support teacher and four aides, a speech language pathologist and four aides, an occupational therapist and four aides, a social worker and an educational psychologist.

Perhaps we'll achieve success, just using Standard English, by dramatically improving current instruction.

Perhaps technology will help, zooming us to the fore.

Perhaps holding off Standard English word-reading and spelling instruction until kids are older, with language enrichment in the first school years, will do the trick.

Perhaps a combination of these factors will work even more effectively.

My firm impression, however, from exploring education in regular-orthography nations and the research base, is that after sensible knowledge-building, we too will implement a fully-regular beginners' orthography that our kids use when first learning to read and write.

And then we'll soar.

We'll take on that beginners' orthography because it's such a practical, inexpensive way to gain enormous advantages:
- Easy, expedited, early-literacy development.
- Our children being strong independent learners.
- Reading difficulties reduced to vastly smaller levels.
- Our schools having ample time.
- Much easier subject-area teaching and learning.
- High literacy levels across Australia.
- Major budget savings due to education working well.

We'll take on that beginners' orthography because we'll find our current time-pressure untenable, once we know how time-rich schools in regular-orthography nations are.

We'll do it too, because we'll find it too difficult and too resource-intensive to achieve easy, equitable, rapid early-literacy development using Standard English for our lower-third, and particularly our lowest-tenth word readers.

Change 7: Insist on Easier Literacy Development

Change 7 really is pivotal, if we're to improve exponentially: *Insist on easier early-literacy development: Reach regular-orthography nations' achievement levels.*

Let's set the bar ethically high, demanding that our kids have early-literacy development that's as easy and rapid as schools routinely achieve across Taiwan, Japan and China.

Let's also insist that we achieve Finland's and Estonia's GENTLE, and demand we prioritise it here.

Please don't dismiss Change 7 because you find it difficult to imagine us realistically achieving it.

That's just WYSYAIN holding you back.

What you see – our current slowness and struggles – you're assuming is normal. It's not, it's only Anglosphere normal. By international standards, it's appallingly low.

Our future will be immensely different from our present and our past.

Our improvement will be exponential and delightfully impressive.

To achieve it, it's vital we set the bar ethically high.

Indeed, it's a change that we cannot do without!

So let's insist our kids' early-literacy education is made as easy as regular-orthography nations routinely achieve.

Our kids are entitled to it.

Change 8
Investigate Beginners' Orthographies

There is no evidence whatsoever for the belief that the best way to learn to read ... is to learn to read in [Standard English]. It would appear rather that the best way to learn to read ... is to learn to read in the Initial Teaching Alphabet.

Frank Warburton & Vera Southgate[xxxv] (1969)
ITA: An Independent Evaluation, UK review of then widespread use of the Initial Teaching Alphabet (ITA)

The value of an idea lies in the using of it.
Thomas Edison[xxxvi]

Change 8 states, *Investigate the potential of beginners' orthographies: Research shows they're key.*

Starting kids on a fully-regular orthography when first learning to read and write creates impressive advantages. Not least, these include having

- Highly-successful, easy, rapid early-literacy development for virtually all children.
- Very few struggling word-readers and writers.
- Highly successful remediation.

- Easier, stronger subject-area learning.
- Greatly reduced time-pressure.
- Markedly reduced expense.

In very strong contrast, we experience huge disadvantages in all of these areas, due to starting our poor wee joeys on Standard English, without a beginners' orthography.

It's therefore extremely important that we consider and investigate fully-regular English beginners' orthographies and their potential, as a key part of our knowledge-building towards educational improvement.

The Benefits are Very Strong Positives

In seminars I present, I often say,

Imagine this: if by the end of Year 2, all kids could read and write every word in every text and were comfortably confident, independent readers and writers, some reading and writing a little more slowly than others, but everyone confident and independent, not needing help.
And if slower-progress kids had responded so effectively to early intervention that they too were powering on.
Wouldn't it be lovely!

And everyone laughs, reflecting on the delightfulness yet impossibility of that scenario, it being unimaginable.

But that delightfulness is NOT an impossibility. We're just WYSYAINing, thinking that our norm of extremely-slow, hard-won word-reading, spelling and early-literacy is the norm elsewhere, and that all nations must be experiencing similar struggles.

That delightfulness is also logical, because highly-regular orthographies make it so easy to learn to read and write.

The evidence is in: if we're thinking that way, we're wrong.

What I described above is reality for kids and teachers in the world's many regular-orthography nations, e.g., Wales, Estonia, Finland, Netherlands, South Korea, Greece, Italy, Poland, Spain, Iceland, Norway, Sweden and Turkey.

Change 8 Investigate Beginners' Orthographies

It's reality too in Taiwan, Japan and China, our role models for introducing beginners' orthographies. To combat the severely disadvantaging impacts of using just their complex orthographies, they introduced their fully-regular beginners' orthographies, to ease and speed early-literacy development, and build powerful learning skills for kids then transitioning to, and mastering, reading and writing of their complex orthographies.

It doesn't take long: just 10 weeks in Taiwan. As researchers Huang and Hanley[xxxvii] (1997) explain,

Before they are taught any characters in school, all Taiwanese children learn a system known as Zhuyin Fuhao, an alphabetic script similar to Pinyin, the alphabetic system used in mainland China.

In Zhuyin Fuhao, each phoneme is represented by a unique visual symbol (in Pinyin, the written symbols comprise letters from the Roman alphabet). There is a total of 37 symbols.

Zhuyin Fuhao is taught during the first 10 weeks of the 1st grade in Taiwan ...

It is not permitted to teach any [Taiwanese] characters during [this time]. The only teaching material is a textbook of the [Taiwanese] language (the first volume) concerned with Zhuyin Fuhao ...

After 10 weeks, the children learn [Taiwanese Hanzi characters] via Zhuyin Fuhao. A representation of the pronunciation of the appropriate word written in Zhuyin Fuhao appears on the right side of the characters in primary school textbooks.

Knowing Zhuyin Fuhao thus helps children to pronounce new characters ... without assistance from the teacher.

Many regular-orthography nations don't use word-reading accuracy tests of word-reading accuracy from Year 2 on – because virtually all kids are fully accurate.

Instead, they use fluency tests, monitoring how quickly and efficiently children read, as fluency builds across the years.

And while a very small number of children in regular-orthography nations do have word-reading and spelling difficulties, their difficulties are extremely minor relative to the severe struggles so many of our cute koala kids endure.

Learning to read a regular-orthography also generates stronger cognitive-processing skills, somewhat akin to the skills that multilingual children develop. Not surprisingly, in PIRLS and PISA, highest-achieving nations have regular orthographies, multilingualism or both.

Findings of research studies of children learning to read in regular-orthography nations are impressive, e.g.,

- Regular-orthography children become proficiently accurate word-readers in Grade 1; Standard English readers are well below that level many years later.
- Regular-orthography children with Down Syndrome and severe intellectual disability have word-reading as accurate as neurotypical 7-year-olds, i.e., with close to full accuracy though not as fast as 10-year-olds.
- Regular-orthography word-reading and spelling difficulties are minor, e.g., with regular-orthography struggling readers reading 3-syllable unfamiliar words better than English struggling readers could read 1-syllable ones; and making very few vowel errors, in contrast to hundreds by English struggling readers.
- Regular-orthography kids read both familiar and unfamiliar words strongly, and don't struggle with unfamiliar words, as Standard English kids do.

More research is needed, and we need Australian research and education to take a strategic role in this research.

Book 2 of the *Aussie Reading Woes* trilogy, *The Research Tours: The Impacts of Orthographic Disadvantage*, explores key studies and research areas, and suggests research directions we might take in building needed knowledge.

The Initial Teaching Alphabet (ITA) Research

We're extremely fortunate that there's copious research on the impressive effectiveness of the Initial Teaching Alphabet (ITA): the English beginners' orthography that Anglosphere trialled with 5-year-olds across the 1960s.

The ITA studies show consistent impressive findings of
- Expedited word-reading and writing development.
- Kids soon being confident, independent, enthusiastic readers and writers.
- Extremely easy transitioning to Standard English.
- Strong Success Inoculation and resilience building.
- Strong boosting of language skills.
- Strong success for slower-progress learners.
- Far fewer children having word-reading and writing difficulties, with these difficulties easy to remediate.
- Highly effective word-reading remediation of older children and adult struggling readers, who'd learned to read and write using solely Standard English.

Those findings are echoed across the myriads of 1960s ITA studies when use of ITA prior to Standard English was explored in many hundreds of studies, large and small, in England, USA, Canada, and even, to a tiny extent, here in Australia.

Here's my favourite ITA quote: a comment a teacher made in the UK's 1966 major review of ITA usage, by Warburton and Southgate[xxxviii] (1969):

The long uphill grind has been cut out. Reading is more an ordinary part of childhood instead of a chore and so the kids take it in their stride. They pick up a book in their free time as they would a paintbrush or jigsaw.

Oh how we'd love early-literacy to be like that here.

The ITA research ended abruptly, unfortunately, when Whole Language philosophy was sweeping the world. Whole Language emphasised engaged reading and reading-comprehension as the keys to healthy reading development, with word-reading positioned as somewhat inconsequential.

With word-reading considered of little importance, so was ITA and its research.

It really is tragic for our kids of the last six decades, and particularly our struggling readers, that ITA was rejected, with its research then ignored. Had ITA been embraced, and integrated into Whole Language, they'd together have ushered in a powerful new paradigm of rich, expansive, Anglophone education success.

The ITA research's sudden end meant intended studies didn't happen, e.g., studies exploring the best timing for transitioning, and optimising of post-transition learning. With those ITA studies not completed, for answers to those issues, we must look to regular-orthography nation research.

Importantly, the extensive ITA studies do show how easily and effectively a fully-regular beginners' orthography can expedite early-literacy development, and reduce both the number of struggling readers and the extent of their difficulties. Their findings also introduce a few bunyips.

The ITA researchers were well aware of the strong negative effects of using solely Standard English. As Professor Sir Cyril Burt[xxxix] said in the UK review's foreword,

Reading is by far the most important subject that the young child learnt at school. It is also the most difficult to teach. 'One in six of our boys and girls', so a recent report assures us, 'leaves school unable to read as that phrase is ordinarily understood – a higher proportion than any other civilised country.'
Nor are the reasons far to seek. English, owing to its composite origin, partly Anglo-Saxon, partly Norman-French, with later borrowings from a dozen different tongues, has a more erratic orthography than any other contemporary language.

Using just one ITA study as an example, here are research findings detailed in Mazurkiewicz's[xl] 1973 report of an 11-year study of 14,000 USA kids, half in ITA classes, and half in Standard English classes:

The advantages of i.t.a. are that it permits the child to:
- *advance more rapidly in reading and writing experience;*
- *achieve significantly superior reading skills at an earlier time;*
- *read more widely;*
- *write more prolifically, more extensively, and with a higher degree of proficiency;*

- *develop high spelling skills fairly early;*
- *show a lack of the inhibitions in writing which are commonly found early in the first year; and*
- *write more creatively in terms of the number of running words and the number of polysyllabic words used.*

An analysis of subsidiary characteristics indicated:
- *a marked reduction in letter confusions;*
- *fewer restrictions on adhering to [school reading books];*
- *reduction in the need for remedial reading, and*
- *a reduction in failure rate.*

Mazurkiewicz[xli] also comments,

The most dramatic flowering of all is evident in the large numbers of free, self-expressive six-year-old writers. They write more abundantly and about many more subjects than do children learning the traditional alphabet. They write alone, without help or editing from teachers, sounding-out their own spellings and using any words they feel like using in any sentence pattern that occurs to them.

Nice, very nice. We'd like that. Rainbows, not bleak grey.

Equally inspiring is the impressive ease kids experienced transitioning from ITA to Standard English. They still had learning to do, but were strongly empowered and ready for it, through the strategic advantages they'd developed:

- Having confident, successful ITA literacy prior to transitioning.
- Being confident learners through the highly successful learning they'd experienced and enjoyed.
- Having strengthened cognitive-processing skills that empowered mastering of Standard English.
- Learning being easy because so many syllables and words are identical in ITA and Standard English.
- Kids being enthusiastic and ready to explore Standard English's many and varied spelling patterns.

In the future, our kids could be that way too.

It's Time for In-Depth Knowledge-Building

We really must do thorough knowledge-building on the potential that fully-regular beginners' orthographies have for expediting the early-literacy development of Australian kids. Ignoring this area would be tragic.

We'd Read the Research

Before doing our own regular-orthography research, we'd of course read widely to explore findings of previous research.

There's value in us reading deeply in three research areas:
- The extensive 1960s Initial Teaching Alphabet (ITA) research that England, USA and Canada conducted.
- Research on word-reading and literacy development in regular-orthography nations, and studies comparing Standard English and regular-orthography readers.
- Intervention studies of Anglophone and regular-orthography weakest word-readers, comparing the extent of progress made.

Reading in these three key areas would give a clearer sense of the major advantages of using a beginners' orthography initially. It would also show how difficult and expensive it's likely to be for our schools to routinely achieve robust word-reading development in our lower-third and lowest-tenth word-readers while we use solely Standard English.

A 2017 paper by our CQU team, *Managing cognitive load as the key to literacy development: Research directions suggested by crosslinguistic research and research on the Initial Teaching Alphabet (ITA),* summarises the research on the Initial Teaching Alphabet, crosslinguistic research of recent decades, and how very challenging it is to achieve lasting, healthy word-reading in struggling readers when using solely Standard English.

It's available on ResearchGate, and is useful reading for folk wanting more detail on these areas. It references key studies that readers might explore in further reading.

The Research Tours explores research that shows lowest-tenth word-readers in regular-orthography nations make impressive progress, while that's far from the case for Standard-English lowest-tenth and weakest word-readers. Alas, the Anglosphere finds our long sad tail of struggling word-readers and spellers extremely difficult to catch-up.

Importantly, regular-orthography nations' studies of their lowest-tenth include kids with other disabilities, and these kids make great progress. In contrast, many Anglophone studies of intervention with weak word-readers only include kids with healthy intellectual skills and no other difficulties. They exclude any weak word-readers who have autism, or behaviour or attention difficulties – which isn't real life for our schools. That's a sobering bunyip.

Even despite this, when Anglophone studies use expert, intensive, ongoing word-reading intervention and all the kids in those studies have healthy intellectual, behaviour and attention skills, the studies consistently show that many kids make sadly minimal progress. More bunyips.

Given that Australian schools are far more complex than research circumstances, and must teach all cute koala kids, including many with multiple disabilities, the intervention research on Standard-English word-readers is sobering.

The difficulties of our severely struggling word-readers – our most at-risk cute koalas – seem perhaps the highest cost of using Standard English as our only orthography.

Now that's a grief-worthy bunyip – and immensely unfair.

We'd Do the Research Needed

Of course, Australian education wouldn't simply launch into trialling a beginners' orthography. We'd do the necessary knowledge-building first.

We'd study development of word-reading, spelling and early-literacy skills both here and in regular-orthography nations. We'd consider the full range of kids, with particular focus on at-risk kids: the lower-third, lowest-tenth and the lowest 2% and 5% of word-readers.

We'd study the development of language skills, both before and after word-reading development, as rapid, easily won early-literacy development can powerfully boost vocabulary and language-skills development. We'd also study the effectiveness of subject-area learning.

We'd include strong focus on cognitive-processing skills including executive-function, orthographic-awareness and phonological-awareness skills, as learning to read and write a regular-orthography enhances their development.

In particular, we'd explore kids' development of phonemic awareness: skills used in hearing and working with the individual sounds of syllables and words.

Our struggling word-readers almost invariably have major phonemic-awareness weakness – and this sadly impedes word-reading and spelling development. Meanwhile, kids in regular-orthography nations develop proficient phonemic awareness very rapidly, in the few weeks to months it takes for them to learn to read and write words.

We'd love our at-risk kids to have this heightened phonemic awareness when they're learning to read and write Standard English, particularly given that, nicely, it is accompanied by heightened cognitive-processing skills.

That's a key advantage of reading and writing a beginners' orthography initially – the powerful literacy and cognitive-processing skills kids build, which then empower mastering of their complex orthography.

In addition, we'd study the word-reading and early-literacy development of kids with intellectual disability, here and in regular-orthography nations. We'd explore their reading and writing progress, and its impacts on life and learning.

It does seem immensely unfair that Australian kids with intellectual disability so often miss out on mastering reading and writing, when that's so often not the case for kids in regular-orthography nations.

We'd explore the supports the regular-orthography kids need, and their speed of early-literacy development.

We'd also explore how their quickly acquired reading and writing advantages them in other areas.

We'd also explore the characteristics of English beginners' orthographies, exploring ITA, Fleksispel with its multiple transitioning stages, and other English orthographies.

Learning from Our Regular-Orthography Schools

Interestingly, Australia already has a large number of schools using regular orthographies. That's very good news.

Orthographies for Aboriginal and Torres Strait Islander languages are mostly highly regular. They were created by missionary societies that prioritised orthographies being regular, to be quick and easy to learn to read and write.

We've also many schools in isolated Aboriginal communities where, prior to starting school, children largely speak their first language, and have only limited exposure to English.

Unfortunately, in those isolated communities, it seems, for the most part, that kids learn to read and write Standard English first, rather than their first language with its fully-regular orthography. From many perspectives, that seems the wrong way round, particularly as many kids have had only minimal exposure to English prior to starting school.

Regular orthographies are very powerful tools for second language learning, in addition to empowering learning to read and write. Where a fully-regular orthography matched to our indigenous kids' spoken first language is available, there's enormous value in kids first learning to read and write their own language to reap the benefits of their highly-regular orthography. That's far better than starting school and early-literacy development with major struggles with both spoken English and English orthographic complexity.

Using their regular-orthography first, while children were learning to read and write, they could also be saturated in English as a second language for listening and speaking. Then with strong, confident early-literacy skills, plus rich phonological, orthographic and cognitive-processing skills they've built through reading and writing their regular orthography, the kids would then be powerfully positioned to learn to read and write Standard English.

We've a long sad history of disadvantaging our first Aussies and, currently, we fail to meet our teaching challenges for them with appallingly monotonous regularity.

It's time to move away from our nasty NAPLAN, PIRLS and PISA pattern of so many of our indigenous cohort being among our lowest achievers. We also need to move away from having far too many of our indigenous kids becoming seriously disadvantaged adults.

Providing effective literacy from earliest school days, then a strong education, seems a sensible, powerful tool that can expedite progress across many aspects of life.

We'd also benefit from wide highlighting and showcasing of indigenous languages and their regular orthographies, as they've potential to enrich all Aussies. In early-childhood enrichment, perhaps via a TV series, crowds of cute koala kids could engage in rich, play-based learning emphasising an indigenous language, absorbing culture while learning to speak, read and write that indigenous language.

Researching in Our Bilingual Schools

Having regular orthographies so close to home offers exciting research and learning opportunities, e.g., studies exploring our indigenous kids' regular-orthography and Standard-English literacy and language-skill levels would be useful in many ways.

In addition to our indigenous bilingual schools, we've other bilingual schools where kids learn to read and write both Standard English and the orthography of the language they are speaking, or learning to speak, e.g., Greek or Italian.

For research purposes, the orthographies used in bilingual schools have a useful range of orthographic complexity, e.g., they include

- Extremely regular Aboriginal orthographies.
- Extremely regular Greek and Italian.
- Extremely regular Hebrew, which then becomes somewhat less regular in middle primary school, when kids' move from pointed to unpointed Hebrew, which omits considerable orthographic information.

- Moderately regular German, which is fully regular for reading, and slightly less so for spelling.
- Somewhat regular French and Danish, which are considerably more regular than Standard English.
- Dual orthographies, Taiwanese, Japanese and Chinese, with children first reading just the fully-regular orthography, then transitioning to their complex orthography.

Into the future, we'll learn a great deal if we encourage collaborative research across our multilingual schools.

Change 8: Explore Beginners' Orthographies

Standard English's abysmal lack of one-to-one Grapheme-Phoneme-Correspondences (GPCs) is in many ways our downfall for our beginning readers.

It creates orthographic confusion; time-consuming, complex learning; excessively drawn-out word-reading and spelling development; floods of struggling readers; and our severe orthographic disadvantage.

This complexity and confusion can be avoided for our kids, with learning and early-literacy progress dramatically eased and speeded, if we first use a beginners' orthography, with its wonderfully consistent, one-to-one GPCs, and thus also build powerful early-literacy and learning skills in our kids, before we transition them to Standard English.

Towards easing and speeding early-literacy development, and having ample teaching and learning time, Change 8 is pivotally important: *Investigate the potential of beginners' orthographies: Research shows they're key.*

Let's do that, starting by exploring how effectively beginners' orthographies work, here and in nations that currently use them, plus deeply exploring the ITA research.

To do anything less would be to do our Aussie kids and Australian education an immense and harsh disservice.

Change 9
Play to Enrich
Language and Learning

To the art of working well a civilized race would add the art of playing well.

George Santayana[xlii]

It is paradoxical that many educators and parents still differentiate between a time for learning and a time for play without seeing the vital connection between them.

Leo F. Buscaglia[xliii]

Change 9 states, *First, play to learn: Start Standard English word-reading instruction from mid-Year 2.*

Let's delay starting formal reading and maths instruction by 2.5 years, until mid-Year 2, and fill the first 2.5 school years with play-based language and learning enrichment.

In doing so, we'd win, win and win:
- We'd overcome our language-weakness epidemic.
- Our kids would develop strong learning readiness.
- Far fewer would become struggling learners, and their difficulties would be considerably more minor.
- Our kids would love learning, and be far more effective, motivated and engaged learners.

There's strong value in this change target. We very much need our joeys to be playing and learning richly.

We Start Too Young

Australia is an isolated nation, and this can cause our education expectations to be somewhat insular. WYSYAIN can then happen all too easily: we assume what happens in education here is the norm in many nations, and thus something to be both expected and accepted.

We're often wrong in that assumption, and need our ABCs.

We WYSYAIN about the age our cute koalas should start learning to read and write. We're used to our kids working hard at school from age 4.5 to 5 years, so we might expect that it's normal and healthy. We're probably wrong.

Most European nations don't start formal education until their kids are at least 7-years-old.

We tend to assume we're rather like European nations as regards raising kids, with similarly gentle and kind child-raising and education.

But just go and visit kindergartens and schools in Finland and Estonia, and you'll soon realise that we're actually rather harsh in how we're treating our 4 to 7-year-olds, insisting they grow up very fast, very young.

We treat 7 and 8-year-olds as big kids here, but in regular-orthography European nations, kids that age are in so many ways still gently nurtured. Those kids are probably appropriately supported, with us the bad guys, forcing our kids to grow up too quickly and too soon.

Given we're kind, benevolent folk who want what's best for our kids, let's use those European nations as role models.

Let's hold back formal instruction till mid-Year 2 for the *Three Rs* – reading, 'riting and 'rithmetic.

We'd still start school at our usual age. Our change would be in the focus of our first 2.5 school years, Prep to mid-Year 2. We would change to using strongly play-based learning, enriching language, literacy, numeracy, social awareness, thinking, cognitive-processing and learning skills.

Along the way we'd cover many early-years Science and Humanities topics. Kids would also explore life through literature – wonderful illustrated children's books our early-years classes would revel in, enjoying rich exploration of children's literature, fairy tales, nursery rhymes and poems.

Of course, this is not to suggest that no children would learn to read during this time, simply that we'd start formal word-reading instruction at mid-Year 2.

Approximately half of Finnish kids are already reading when they start Grade 1 and formal reading instruction. In similar manner, many of our cute koala kids would also start reading earlier, as part of playing to learn.

Just as Finland and Estonia do with their 6 to 7-year-old Kindergarten kids, there's value in our kids playing with letters and their sounds in play-based contexts from mid-Year 1. Perhaps we'd reduce kids' workload as European nations do, by initially using just all lowercase letters (*cat*, but not *Cat* or *CAT*), or all capitals (*CAT*) until children are reading confidently. The Initial Teaching Alphabet (ITA) uses just lowercase letters, while Finland and Estonia initially just use capitals.

So, yes, our kids would likely be learning letter-sounds, but in play-based learning from age 6, not as a *must* at age 4.5 to 5 years. And yes, some kids would do wonderful reading and writing in those first 2.5 years – in developmentally-appropriate, relaxed, investigative, play-based learning.

Similarly, we'd have strong play-based engagement with early maths concepts, with our joeys building skills with size, volume, measurement and numbers, counting to 10 and back, and so on. Most definitely, our cute koala, budding mathematicians would soon have advanced skills.

All of this would be part of healthy, playful, often child-directed, GENTLE learning, adeptly guided by teachers and teacher aides. It's what our early-childhood educators would love to be doing, and have done so well in decades past.

Let's End Our Language-Weakness Epidemic

I'm not just being warm and fuzzy here, saying we must let the children play. Our language-weakness epidemic is serious and must be resolved in our improving of education.

Australian education desperately needs those first 2.5 years used strategically if early-literacy development is to go well for our at-risk kids.

Adding in 2.5 years of language enrichment and holding back formal word-reading instruction is an astute tactical move that's much needed, if we're to close our Early Years Factory and remove the major deprivations we have due to starting formal word-reading instruction too soon.

The language skills school-aged children use include rich levels of receptive and expressive vocabulary, listening comprehension, language expression, language reasoning, pragmatic (social) reasoning, inferencing and thinking.

They also include cognitive-processing skills, including executive-function skills, short-term and working memory, orthographic awareness and phonological awareness: skills for thinking about words, syllables, rimes (the parts that rhyme) and phonemes (words' individual sounds).

These language subskills play essential roles in Standard English early-literacy and learning development.

Currently, in Australia, our epidemic of language weakness means we've a vast swathe of cute koala joeys starting school severely at-risk of literacy and learning failure because of their too fledgling language skills.

Many are also at-risk of major behavioural, attention and socialisation difficulties. These little Aussies, our future, desperately need our support.

As Geoff Masters[xliv] emphasises, in *Five challenges for Australian school education*,

> There are twin challenges:
> - *To support and promote the progress of all children – and particularly children who lag in their development in the preschool years; and*

- To ensure that all children make a smooth transition into the first year of school by meeting their individual points of need on entry.

That's so true. Too many cute koala joeys start school at such high risk that it's almost guaranteed they'll develop major literacy difficulties. Furthermore, all our kids are ready to learn: the problem is our schools aren't sufficiently resourced and can't provide the tailored supports many kids need.

Combining weak language skills with English orthographic complexity, a very young starting age, and largely one-size-fits-all instruction, sets all too many Aussie kids odds-on for ongoing literacy and learning struggles.

We need to stop that.

As Jackie French[xlv] wisely said, in our mantra for change,
*There are no such things as reading difficulties.
There are only teaching challenges.*

For too many kids, we fail to meet our teaching challenges from the day they start school. It's our schooling practices that we need to change, so we meet our teaching challenges effectively for every cute koala joey from start of school.

Ending Deprivations from Starting Too Soon

We make education so much harder when we start reading, writing and maths instruction when many children are too young. Even more so when our conveyor belt of Australian Curriculum expectations drags learning inexorably on.

For many at-risk kids, the learning soon becomes too hard, with our Early Years Factory then impacting them in nasty ways. Our at-risk but nonetheless cool, confident, destined-for-success, cute koala joeys first become subdued ... then concerned ... then struggling ... and are sadly crushed and crumpled by the time the factory spits them out.

Let's consider some of the major deprivations we create by starting formal word-reading instruction too soon.

Deprivation 1: Reduced Intervention Opportunities

By starting so early, we reduce opportunities for effective early-childhood intervention. Why? Because our pre-school koala joeys are too immature for that intervention.

Many at-risk kids need several years of readiness building. Now, there's lots of great intervention you can do with 4.5 to 5-year-olds, and lots more still when formal word-reading instruction is still years away at mid-Year 2.

But you can't do that same intervention with 3-year-olds. It's also difficult to identify 3-year-olds at definite risk of struggles, whereas that's easy when kids are 5-year-olds.

Deprivation 2: We Can't Fit In Building of Readiness

By starting so early, our schools can't fit in the effective readiness building and early intervention that so many of our joeys need before they start formal word-reading and spelling instruction. Our teachers are only given weeks and months, and for crowds of joeys, that's woefully insufficient, given they're heading for solely Standard English.

In so many cases, our schools fail to meet their teaching challenges not due to lack of effort, but because there's far too little time to provide the extent of supports kids need.

Deprivation 3: Too Complex Learning Is Time Consuming

We slow learning and make it far more drawn-out, hugely exacerbating our resourcing needs, when we choose to teach very complex content to very young children.

Compared to 7 and 8-year-olds, 4.5 to 5-year-old kids are woefully immature. The complex learning we demand of our kids would take far less time, if done when they were older.

Deprivation 4: We Reduce Kids' Pre-School Time

In European regular-orthography nations, there's ample time for parents and childcare centres to provide masses of rich literacy and literacy experiences, right up until the kids are starting Grade 1, aged 7 and 8-years-old.

We sadly reduce opportunities for families to enrich kids when we start formal reading instruction at 4.5 to 5 years.

In starting formal instruction so young, we vastly reduce the opportunities that kids' families have to build rich literacy readiness before kids start school and learning to read.

Literate Cultural Capital is kids' *backpacks* of rich early-childhood literacy experiences, and readiness for literacy learning that they've built at home, and bring to school.

This bank of early-literacy experiences – kids being read to, talking about books, and doing rich imaginative *What if ...* thinking, extending from those books – is both incredibly valuable and hugely important.

Deprivation 5: We Activate Risk Factors

When we start word-reading instruction so young, and use solely Standard English, we greatly increase the number of risk factors that become activated, with these subsequently derailing kids across their Early Years Factory years. Importantly, many of these risk factors we activate here aren't risk factors for kids who are older, or who learn to read a beginners' orthography.

As an example, phonological awareness, working memory and cognitive-processing skills increase considerably from age 5 to 7 years. Young children with weakness in these skills at age 5 years are sitting ducks for Standard English literacy struggles, but might well thrive if we started later, after 2.5 years of language enrichment, and even more so if we used a beginners' orthography.

I'll stop there at five deprivations, as I'm sure you get the picture. I could easily add more.

Let's Do 2.5 Years of Language Enrichment

By holding back formal literacy and numeracy instruction, our first 2.5 years of schooling could become a wonderful time of rich language, literacy and learning development for all our cute koala joeys.

Let's aim for all kids to have at least 50 favourite books and rhymes in their metaphorical backpacks by mid-Year 2 – texts they're passionate about and keen to discuss at length.

Fifty might seem a lot but it's not – some nursery rhymes, alphabet and counting songs, some fairy tales and poems, plus many wonderful books. These texts, which kids will be highly familiar with, could then be used in powerful ways in literacy learning across the primary-school years.

We want strong focused-attention and executive-function skills too, and to ensure kids have Successful Engaged Learning. Enjoyed learning using literature experiences can build those skills and ensure the success that's needed.

Further, we want our cute koalas to be confident, proficient listeners, skilled at taking in auditory information, thinking it over, and acting on it.

We also want kids keenly following the first instruction their teachers give. Currently, in every year-level, too many kids are incredibly poor listeners, not focusing sufficiently on instructions and information their teachers provide. They half listen as the teacher explains tasks to the class, then want it explained personally: "*What do I do, Miss?*".

This poor listening multiplied by several million cute koalas, year after year after year, insidiously reduces learning time in all our year-levels, from Prep to Year 12.

Turning that issue around, so our kids are keen listeners who follow the first instruction, would impressively improve teaching and learning time.

Poor listening in class doesn't seem nearly as big an issue in regular-orthography nations, e.g., daydreaming was the biggest issue listed in one international study *The Research Tours* discusses.

We also need and want kids to love rich words and phrases: weak vocabulary at age 2.5 years predicts school struggles.

Let's cut that inevitability off at the pass. We can, but only when we have ample time to enrich language and learning.

We want our kids to be word and phrase finders, collectors of wonderful rich words and sayings that they find in books and hear elsewhere.

We also want our kids to be proficient conversationalists, participating confidently and philosophically in discussions, as topics are explored. Frequent, long conversational dyads are vitally important in our building of thoughtful Aussies: *I talk, then you talk, then we pause and think, then I comment, then you discuss* ... and on it goes.

Too many joeys have had too few conversational dyads when they start school. They benefit much from modelling of active listening and conversing, then fun practising of these skills.

Of course, we also want to boost our kids' imaginations through the many and varied wonderful formats, activities and themes that early-childhood educators love. There's definitely no need to go to Finland or Estonia for ideas on this area. Our early childhood educators have these skills in abundance, and would so love to be using them.

That 2.5 years of play-based language enrichment will most definitely not be time wasted. It will instead richly invest in our future, at child, school and national level.

Let's Measure and Monitor Language Skills

While we're enriching all kids in many ways, play-based intervention efficiently provided by allied-health staff, including trained aides, will also be the order of the day for our many cute koala kids in need of it.

As part of that, we need to systematically test and monitor kids' language-skills development, before school, at start of school, and across the school years.

Systematic screening of diverse communication, play and interaction skills at the start of school, along with hearing, vision, coordination and socialisation skills, would identify joeys needing additional supports and tailored intervention. They'd then be provided with the allied-health intervention that's needed, including speech language pathology and occupational therapy, counselling and mentoring.

Kids' cognitive-processing skills can also be quickly and easily assessed, including short-term and working memory, key executive-function skills, phonological awareness and also Rapid Automised Naming (RAN): a handy measure of ability to rapidly retrieve concepts from long-term memory and activate them. Kids weak in these cognitive-processing skills are highly at-risk of developing Standard English word-reading and spelling struggles. They need strategic play-based intervention, building literacy readiness skills.

It's important we avoid excessive assessment and use practical, tailored assessment, preferably using quick, easy-to-use, highly-engaging tasks kids enjoy, which provide the information we need to guide instruction and interventions.

In that tailoring, we'd ensure less-frequent, less-detailed testing of healthy-progress kids, and more-detailed testing and monitoring of skill development in our kids with weak skills, who need and will benefit from appropriate boosting.

It's also very important that this testing isn't added to class-teachers' workload. Our teachers and teachers' unions often scream loudly when extra testing is recommended. That's logical, and quite understandable, as time spent testing is time not spent teaching, and test administration and scoring can add considerable administrative load.

The increased learning-support and allied-health contingent that I've recommended for our schools, for every 500 enrolled students, could play a huge role in this knowledge-building.

Further, it's likely that time spent testing and doing test administration will reduce increasingly into the future, as computerised testing becomes increasingly efficient, with results generated quickly and easily.

Play-Based Resilience for Later Word-Reading

We'd be able to build both resilience and readiness for later Standard-English learning in our kids, using strategic play-based teaching of small units of key word-reading skills. This is easy to do and can have very powerful positive impacts.

While we're not yet using a beginners' orthography, play-based learning from Prep to Year 2 would include kids learning beginners' sightwords: words recognised instantly, on sight. They'd learn to read their names, then perhaps the names of a few class puppets whose hilarious antics are incorporated in fun, class books.

They'd label their world, writing word labels to put up in the classroom and at home. Kids might then learn family names: *Mum, Dad, Smith, Gran, Sophie, Jack* and *Louis,* and have labels with family members' names on, which they'd choose from, when deciding which lucky family members get today's great artworks that they've made.

Too often, the first sightwords schools teach are abstract words such as *a, to, for, and, it, in,* words which many joeys have little awareness of. The kids instead need to learn a small set of concrete relevant words they easily identify with, such as *dinosaur, car, plane, bus, train, boat, dog, cat, run, play, jump, hide,* and names of friends and family.

Fun strategic learning of first sightwords doesn't just build word-reading readiness. It's Success Inoculation, which can decrease kids' likelihood of Acquired Helplessness. It's also dynamic assessment: a powerful way to identify kids at-risk of later sightword difficulties. These kids would then enjoy strategic play that's relatively adult-directed – what we might call intervention, but kids call fun. This would ensure that those early sightwords are confidently mastered, readying the kids for formal word-reading instruction they'll meet in future years, and greatly reducing likelihood of struggles in that learning.

Mastering a tiny set of sightwords can be powerful in building resilience, readying kids for when they're later learning to read and write our complex Standard English. This small set of learning can be very powerful in moving kids from at-risk to strong success in reading and writing.

Our kids would also play with letters, initially learning the letter at the start of their names, and then a strategic small group of perhaps five to seven consonants and vowels.

My book *Phonological Fun,* does this, developing resilience for learning to read and write Standard English, through building word-reading readiness: confidence and skill with syllables, rhyming and phonemic awareness, and a small group of letters and their sounds. It uses rhyme, syllable and sound characters, and seven letters, *b m f s t* and *a o*, each having a letter character – *Beebubee, Memmummem* and so on, with each name emphasising its letter's sound.

That tiny letter set can then be used very strategically, e.g., with kids playing with moon-monster names, e.g., *om, ob, am, fot, sab*, for moon-monster artworks created in class that day. The word-making they enjoy with that tiny letter set will build resilience and readiness for later learning.

In this pre-word-reading play, again, teachers would be on the look-out for kids at-risk. Assessment often doesn't need to use detailed formal tests: in so many instances, using dynamic assessment works extremely well.

Observing kids' skills and confidence in pre-literacy game activities soon reveals kids who show signs of weakness. Once identified, they can engage in play-based intervention that ensures successful learning, and readies them for stronger word-reading development in future years.

Teacher-led conversations about words would explain our three types of words and syllables, and build kids' awareness of and metacognition about *Regular, Pattern* and *Tricky* words and syllables:

- *Regular* ones we sound-out, e.g., *bus, cat, vet* and moon monster names *om, ob, am, fot, sab*.
- *Pattern* ones that use common patterns kids get to know, as they play with Pattern Words such as *ball, car*, that in turn help them read and write partner pattern words, e.g., *ball-call-small, car-far-jar*, using rhyme. Most kids love playing with rhyme, and for those who don't, schools would build needed subskills that enable rhyming to become easy and fun.
- *Tricky* ones that try to trick us with silly spelling, e.g., *one, two, was*, so we use our *remembering eyes* to recall what they look like. The class might have a Tricky Word Train where kids post Tricky words.

Our kids would also meet Australian English's 20 common vowel-sounds, and play with them, perhaps sorting pictures by listening for the vowel sound of the picture's name, then deciding if its vowel sound is that of, e.g., *car* or *cow*.

In like manner, we'd build maths and numeracy readiness, by giving kids what they need. The emphasis would be on all kids enjoying learning, and progressing well. Learning and activities would be strategic, ensuring kids experience strong Successful Engaged Learning.

And, where it's needed, at-risk joeys would enjoy tailored intervention fun, to the extent needed for healthy progress.

Fun Expands Kids' Working Memory

Anxiety reduces our kids' working memory, while relaxed confidence expands it. Let's ensure we teach to kids who have *fat happy cups* of working memory.

The vast majority of activities I've developed over the years are games: skill-building games that use counters and dice, and packs of cards for strategic Memory and Snap fun.

In using games, I'm not just trying to be nice.

I want to expand kids' working memory and that happens best when kids are relaxed and having fun. I also want their working memory focused firmly on the specific content I'm helping them master. Games with key learning content as their centre of attention can both focus children's attention and maximise their learning.

Games are also a useful means of achieving ample practice, and high *instructional intensity*: kids getting lots of practices of a skill per minute of time. We want kids to have the extent of fun practice that they need, to build skills from fledgling through to mastery and automaticity. Games can be very useful for this purpose.

Fun play-based teaching and learning can strategically support skill development, providing opportunities for careful introduction of skills, then scaffolded learning, and ample practice, along with dynamic assessment – teachers keeping a keen eye out for at-risk cute koalas who need and will benefit from strategic, extra, play-based learning fun.

Our having 2.5 years of strong play-based learning would be a major step forward in our improving of education.

Having ample time, and not being stressed and pressured, would enable highly effective, tailored instruction and intervention that's lots and lots of fun.

Change 9: Play to Enrich Language and Learning

Change 9 is needed: *First, play to learn: Start Standard English word-reading instruction from mid-Year 2.*

It's a sad, mad, bad education world when many 4 and 5-year-old Aussie kids are marked for learning difficulties and long years of struggles simply because we start formal word-reading instruction when they're so young.

That's sad, extremely sad.

For our crushed and crumpled koalas for whom SCHOOL is all too often those Sad Cruel Hours of Our Lives, sadness accumulates. There's lots of sadness, even in one boring hour daily, if it happens five days per week times 40 weeks per year times 13 years of schooling.

That's all too many sad, bad hours, with our kids victims of our education systems' unfortunate choices of age and orthography, and us not meeting our teaching challenges.

Let's change that. Let's instead use our first 2.5 school years for rich, play-based learning that includes copious language and learning enrichment, careful building of readiness, and play-based intervention to the level each at-risk koala needs.

This will enable catching precious Aussies before they fall, and save many from long years of sadness and struggles, especially if we also use a beginners' orthography.

It will also make improving education vastly easier here.

Change 10
Build Useful Research Knowledge

We shall have no better conditions in the future if we are satisfied with all those which we have at present.

Time is really the only capital that any human being has and the thing that he can least afford to waste or lose.

Thomas Edison[xlvi] [xlvii]

Change 10 is *Build needed research knowledge as quickly as possible: Use collaborative school-based research.*

Let's do this: build useful knowledge in the areas where knowledge is currently lacking, and keep that knowledge-building hugely school focused. We've far too many Swiss-cheese research areas that we need to convert to good solid cheddar.

We've considerable research to do and we need to build that research knowledge quickly and efficiently.

Let's Do Research in Australian Schools

Let's do research in Aussie schools, building important knowledge on kids' development of literacy and language skills, plus their information-processing skills, including cognitive-processing, executive-function, phonological and orthographic-awareness, and statistical-learning skills.

Funding for educational research has been sadly low in Australia across the decades, thus we've far too many areas of Swiss-cheese research. We must change that.

I'm looking forward to Australia becoming a leading educational-research nation as we improve both literacy development and education here.

Whilst international research is important and useful as a basis for our learning, we also need Aussie research that establishes our upper and lower-third cute koala kids' skill levels for cognitive processing and literacy skills; and how these skill levels impact each other's development, and create differing instructional needs in our koala thirds.

Australian research is essential because we differ from the USA and UK, where most Anglosphere research is done.

For a start, we've far less school resourcing for early-years instruction and strategic intervention for our struggling readers. It's therefore harder for our teachers to achieve remediation and effectively-differentiated instruction.

Additionally, the USA and UK have strong national focus on systematic word-reading instruction, whereas our decision-making is done more on a school-by-school basis.

Importantly, more than many nations do, we emphasise kids learning to read through extensive engaged reading of texts of manageable difficulty.

There's been amazingly little research on the impacts of engaged reading on word-reading development, yet clearly successful engaged reading is a key factor building many Aussie kids' word-reading and literacy skills. There's value in us researching this area as part of our learning journey.

Because our education here differs from other nations in key ways, we need to reinvent the wheel in strategic ways:
- Replicating selected studies conducted in other nations in Australian school settings.
- Exploring the impact of Aussie reading instruction methods on upper and lower-third kids' literacy levels.

- Exploring how cognitive processing, word-reading, spelling, self-teaching, statistical learning, Success Inoculation and Acquired Helplessness interrelate as word-reading, spelling, reading and writing develop.

Let's Include Consensus Research

Let's become a nation that's known for efficient, effective educational research and knowledge-building, as well as our impressive educational changes and improvement.

Towards building knowledge more quickly and efficiently, let's use a range of research methods.

In *Bridging the Gap*, our CQU team proposed *Consensus Research* as a useful, relatively rapid means of building research knowledge on issues impacting literacy progress.

Conducted as collaborative research with university and teacher researchers working together, Consensus Research involves multiple strategic cycles of knowledge-building.

These cycles would involve teachers, schools and academics engaging in many and varied, individual, small studies, and then considering the findings of those studies.

In each cycle, they'd consider the knowledge gained thus far, discussing findings, offering insights, applying findings to improvement decision-making, and, where needed, deciding upon further projects, to provide additional detail that's needed in key areas.

There is always a place for experimental and quasi-experimental research studies, and qualitative research in its various forms is also immensely valuable. Towards speeding our building of knowledge, we'd probably use many and varied research methods extensively. We'll also use systemic data, e.g., from NAPLAN, and data that teachers and university researchers gather.

We'd also have our Consensus Research studies on key focus areas. While less rigorous individually, collaborative studies and discussions collectively have potential to be of great value, and can build knowledge quickly and efficiently.

The Research Problem

In research, a thesis statement or hypothesis is usually stated, to consider and explore. Here's a useful practical thesis statement for Australian education. It details the struggling-education research problem we both need to and want to resolve, and potential solutions we need to explore:

Australian education is currently insufficiently effective for most students, and grossly ineffective for our lower-third students – our at-risk and struggling readers. Causal factors include English orthographic complexity and its impacts, our beginners' very young age, many children starting school highly at-risk of difficulties, insufficient school resourcing, too high child and teacher workload, and our having too many struggling readers with major difficulties.

Our struggling readers' major instructional needs add additional teacher workload to what is already extremely high workload, making it excessive. This in turn reduces effectiveness of education for all our children, because our teachers are too busy to effectively meet all children's instructional needs.

This complex struggling-education problem can be resolved, and powerful positive changes are possible at relatively low expense, if we explore and implement effective methods used in other nations.

Possible changes include using a fully-regular beginners' orthography when children first learn to read and write, raising our starting age for formal reading instruction, adding in strong play-based language enrichment and allied-health intervention supports prior to formal reading instruction, reducing teacher workload, and providing ample, effective school supports.

These changes have powerful potential to expedite early-literacy development and mastering of Standard English literacy, plus reduce early-literacy difficulties, time pressure and our significantly high child and teacher workload.

These, in turn, can make Australian education both far more effective and considerably less expensive.

Fortunately, strategically focused research is powerful at successfully addressing research problems.

Let's make strategic research focused on the issues in this thesis statement a vital part of Australian education.

In *The Research Tours,* I've proposed 100 research questions that Australian education might explore. They are useful, practical research questions with potential to expedite our knowledge-building, actioning research at a useful range of levels, using both formal and informal research studies.

Resourcing Our Research

Earlier, I listed four important school resourcing items that together could do much towards reducing workload and improving education here:

- Reducing class teachers' in-class hours by perhaps 200 hours annually.
- Providing a full-time teacher aide for every full-time class teacher.
- Increasing our learning-support and allied-health support services.
- Strategically improving the teaching supports provided by our Australian Curriculum developers.

Here, I'm adding four needed items of research resourcing: items that we desperately need, which would strategically and impressively empower our educational research.

Item 1: Increased Research Funding

Our first research investment would be increased annual educational-research funding for the years it takes us to achieve education as effective as regular-orthography nations routinely achieve.

Finland, a tiny nation with a quarter of our population, is an excellent role model for educational-research spending – they're a world leader in funding for educational research.

Not surprisingly, because of this, as *The Research Tours* explores, Finnish research has contributed many useful findings on regular-orthography word-reading and literacy development, instruction and learning, e.g., the *Jyvaskyla Longitudinal Study of Dyslexia* and its research offshoots are exemplary research from which we can learn much.

Further, Australia has saved quite savagely on educational research across recent decades, giving us major needs for catch-up research. More bunyips.

We need to produce solid Aussie cheddar to replace our far too prolific Swiss-cheese research gaps.

Because of our education woes, our research funding needs are exponentially higher than Finland's. With major needs for efficient knowledge-building and, to date, a sad lack of research, and far too many knowledge gaps, a research budget four times higher than Finland's seems in order.

Item 2: A Focused Australian Research Project

Our second research investment is a strategic Australia-wide research project focused on the 10 Changes and associated issues, one which coordinates, resources and supports associated school-level research projects.

University researchers would work together with teacher researchers in schools, both here and in other nations, in collaborative research partnerships. There'd be a range of projects teachers and schools might engage in, choosing projects usefully aligned with their current school priorities.

Item 3: Teacher Researchers

Our third research investment is providing the supports needed so that many of our teachers are active participants in our 10 Changes research, with options of their research involving Graduate Diploma, Masters and Doctoral studies.

Teacher researchers and university researchers working together can be a powerful combination. As other nations do, we'd make these postgraduate studies free of charge, and provide pay incentives for engaging in relevant studies.

We'd also provide time-support, with off-class hours offered at graded levels, e.g., a half-day fortnightly for Graduate Diploma studies, a full-day fortnightly for Masters research studies, and a full-day weekly for Doctoral research studies.

The projects teachers engage in would usually be of definite practical usefulness to their schools, and quite likely, much of this off-class time would be used on school projects.

Teachers, if you've been thinking of perhaps doing Masters or Doctoral studies, the perfect time is now, or soon.

We want and need our teachers to be active participants in our research and knowledge-building. We also want them to continue teaching. It's therefore very important that their total workload is very manageable.

Let's thus amply resource our teacher researchers and schools so researching is welcomed, valued and prioritised.

Item 4: Open Access and Knowledge Sharing

Our fourth research investment is exemplary, open sharing of past, present and future research knowledge.

To date, we've been mushrooming our teachers far too much, keeping them in the dark, often feeding them information that's third, fourth, fifth and even tenth-hand. That's not a wise investment when we want cutting-edge education.

Let's empower our teachers through ready access to online databases of research articles, where abstracts (summaries of articles) can be explored, with relevant articles then easily downloaded for deeper reading, sharing and discussions.

Let's also ensure our My State, My Nation Website that I've suggested, or an associated website, has a research section akin to the USA's *Education Resources Information Centre* (ERIC), which collects research articles and also project information, with these freely available to all readers.

In future research, let's also share on that website ongoing information from our 10 Changes research projects.

We'd include details of proposed and current research projects, and pertinent information from our Consensus Research cycles.

We'd also invite evaluations of project research findings, from schools, teachers and university researchers.

Let's Use Our ABCs, 10 Changes and 2035 Goal

In doing research that builds necessary knowledge towards improvement, let's please keep our ABCs of improving education front and centre. They really are very important:

A. ACT locally while looking globally.

B. BOOST the lower-third to benefit everyone.

C. CHANGE effectively to work less and achieve more.

Using those ABCs, let's build useful knowledge quickly, using collaborative school-centred research:

Change 1

Let's build widespread understanding of how orthographies matter, and how English spelling currently drags us down.

Change 2

Let's build awareness and ownership of our struggling reader woes, the meagre supports our kids receive, and the hypocrisy and pretence that we live with, as regards the school and allied-health supports we currently provide.

Change 3

Let's weigh and compare child and teacher workload and stress-levels, here and in regular-orthography nations.

Change 4

Let's build strong understanding of upper and lower-third readers' very different skill levels, and the differences in tailoring of instruction that are needed for us to meet our teaching challenges effectively for all our cute koala kids.

Change 5

Let's build comprehensive knowledge on Aussie kids' word-reading levels, word-reading's role in literacy development and difficulties, and optimising of word-reading instruction.

Change 6

Let's build thorough knowledge on how we can achieve enriched, tailored education and mentoring efficiently and effectively for each and every Aussie child.

Change 7
Let's build useful knowledge on
- The ethics of our children's so much slower and more arduous word-reading and literacy development, and their higher likelihood of major literacy difficulties.
- The mechanisms and changes needed for us to achieve literacy development as easy and rapid as regular-orthography nations routinely achieve.

Change 8
Let's build knowledge on the potential of using an initial, fully-regular, English beginners' orthography when our kids first learn to read and write.

Change 9
Let's build knowledge towards achieving highly effective play-based language and learning enrichment for our first 2.5 years of schooling.

Change 10
Let's generate needed knowledge quickly and efficiently.

In doing so, let's keep our 2035 goal very much in mind:

> *By 2035, Australian education will be*
> *routinely, efficiently, gently and easily*
> *achieving highly effective, rapid development of*
> *children's word-reading, spelling, writing and*
> *early-literacy skills,*
> *in GENTLE manner,*
> *in every early-years classroom,*
> *in all schools across our nation,*
> *as efficiently as is achieved routinely*
> *across schools in regular-orthography nations*
> *such as Taiwan, Japan and China,*
> *with at least 98% of Australian school children*
> *being confident, independent readers and writers,*
> *able to read 95% of the 10,000 most-frequent words,*
> *by age 8.5 years, or within 18 months of starting*
> *formal word-reading instruction.*

Let's Strategically Research Potential Changes

Our school-based research would have multiple strands that simultaneously build knowledge on many fronts.

Two changes I'm suggesting, which may prove to be pivotal, are important research areas we need to explore:
- Change 8: our initially using a fully-regular beginners' orthography, prior to Standard English.
- Change 9: our holding back the age we start reading instruction, using strategic play-based language and learning enrichment across our first 2.5 school years.

We'd first do preliminary knowledge building, exploring the realities of literacy and learning in schools in regular-orthography nations, while also deeply exploring research literature, including studies *The Research Tours* explores.

Then, we'd benefit by research that includes four strategic strands, so we carefully investigate both the separate and combined benefits of actioning Changes 8 and 9:
1. Working to achieve optimal Standard English word-reading instruction that starts in Prep (Foundation), with all needed resourcing provided.
2. Holding back Standard English instruction until mid-Year 2, with the first 2.5 school years being language and learning enrichment.
3. Using a fully-regular beginners' orthography, and starting word-reading instruction in Prep.
4. Holding back both the beginners' orthography and word-reading instruction until mid-Year 2, with the first 2.5 school years being language and learning enrichment.

At the same time, we'd compare our achievements with those of higher-achieving Anglophone nations such as Canada and Ireland, and regular orthography nations.

Given we've considerable useful information on the Initial Teaching Alphabet (ITA) from the 1960s, let's not spend time exploring lots of beginners' orthographies. Exploring both Fleksispel and ITA, and considering their similarities and differences, along with 1960s studies of options explored in

English beginners' orthographies, will support decision-making as to the beginners' orthographies we would trial.

Change 10: Build Useful Knowledge Quickly

Change 10 is *Build needed research knowledge as quickly as possible: Use collaborative school-based research.*

The expanded research budgets and school resourcing I'm recommending are hugely needed. Our complex, struggling-education problem is entrenched and ongoing, and it will require considerable research effort initially, as we work towards actioning effective solutions.

So let's do this: the practical knowledge-building that's needed, to build our improved education world.

Let's instigate strategic research programs at school-level, here and with other nations.

Let's insist we build this crucially needed knowledge very efficiently, so we achieve, as soon as possible, the easier and faster word-reading and early-literacy development that our cute koalas are entitled to.

Notably, let's insist we meet that challenge for our most at-risk cute koala kids, our lower-third and lowest-tenth word-readers, vulnerable Aussies impacted most severely by our current severe orthographic disadvantage. Let's insist their early-literacy development is as rapid and easy as that of regular-orthography lower-third and lowest-tenth readers.

Let's also insist we build this research knowledge with impressive speed.

PART 3
INTO THE FUTURE WE GO

Let's Work Upstream and Down

Action without vision is only passing time, vision without action is merely day dreaming, but vision with action can change the world.

Nelson Mandela[xlviii]

Picture a rapidly flowing river, wide and deep, the wind rippling small waves across its surface, the opposite bank far away, trees tiny on its shoreline. And as you look out across the water, oh no, you can see koala kids, hordes of cute koala kids, struggling to keep afloat …

… In other words, we've lots of struggling readers.

Quickly, the adults on the shore get to work. On the bank close by, one team using tyres, ropes, and a chain of folk skilled with working with youngsters, is soon pulling joeys from the water. Indeed, the kids seem to be enjoying it …

… In other words, it's wonderful when our early intervention is highly effective.

Further down, a big team seems able to rescue a smaller number of strugglers in life-saving ways …

… In other words, while remediation can be effective, it's usually not as effective as successful early intervention.

Still further downstream, a team with deliberately calm demeanour is pulling exhausted older kids from the water and resuscitating them …

... In other words, many of our kids with entrenched learning difficulties are hugely dispirited, and will need far more extensive supports if they're to get through with healthy coping and literacy skills, as they're highly at-risk of ongoing major literacy and life difficulties.

And fortunately there is a convenient bend in the river after that ...

... In other words, I'm not going to talk about any teams further downstream, because, sigh, life can be dreadful and depressing for our teenagers and adults with severe literacy difficulties, struggling with employment and life.

The teams are working well, and a harmonious sense builds that this is a satisfying status quo ...

... In other words, we've all too much WYSYAIN, given we're not meeting our teaching challenges sufficiently for at least a third of our cute koala kids, and early-literacy development here is nowhere near as good as it needs to be.

Then, to general surprise, along the bank, diverse adults break away from the different teams, and start to head upstream, at first one by one and seeming uncertain, but then talking at length with each other, and becoming more purposeful, intent and excited, as away they stride along the bank, clearly having plans in mind.

"Where are you going?" ring out the panicked voices of the teammates they've left. *"You mustn't leave! The kids are drowning and we've got to rescue them. Stop! We need you here! Stop! Stop!"*

And the voice of those heading upstream is heard, loud and clear, across the wind and waves,
"We're going upstream to work there. We need to work out how to stop our joeys falling in!"

Lessons on Rescuing Koalas from Drowning

It's a good analogy, isn't it? It's not mine, and it's used a lot in public health medicine. I first heard it used in education at a conference in Vancouver, where I was presenting.

This analogy is all about deciding where to seek directions and set our goals.

Can we say what we're doing is good enough? We can't, because one thing international reading studies are good at is showing us our continuing, excessive numbers of low achievers, and how we're struggling.

Additionally, our kids have rights that we're not meeting effectively.

Plus, we're an ethical, moral society that genuinely wants what's best for our kids.

We also need to be able to balance the budget while we're resourcing education effectively.

The goal I've set for Australian education is early-literacy development that's as easy and rapid as schools routinely achieve in Taiwan, Japan and China, and as GENTLE as Finland and Estonia achieve.

That's because all Aussie kids, including at-risk kids, have a right to education as gentle and effective as that achieved routinely in many nations.

I'm thinking you're coming around to that idea, that it really is essential that we set the bar ethically high, if we're to achieve the spectacular progress that we're so capable of.

Aim too low, and that's definitely what we'll achieve.

Ten years should be the maximum time we take in reaching our goal of easy, effective, rapid early-literacy development, with strong progress by the five-year mark.

There are multiple options we need to explore to reach that goal. All of them need serious consideration, prior to being investigated.

Working downstream, we must explore optimising of word-reading and writing instruction and remediation while we use solely Standard English, to establish whether schools can routinely achieve strong word-reading efficiently and effectively in 98% of school kids, by improving instruction.

Working upstream, we need to explore major sociocultural changes, including
- Initially using a fully-regular beginners' orthography, prior to Standard English.
- Using the first 2.5 years for both play-based learning enrichment and intervention.
- Holding back the starting age for formal Standard English word-reading and spelling instruction till kids are older, with stronger learning skills and resilience.

As part of weighing child and teacher workload, we'll study time – the time we use in developing skills, time that's saved for other learning, and the extent of our Find the Learning Time Challenge and Find the Caring Time Challenge.

Doubtless there are other useful options to also explore, as education is far broader than the issues I've raised.

Nonetheless, to be equitable and ethical, some actions are imperative. Into the future, we simply must
- Stop our cute koalas from falling into that river of Standard English literacy struggles.
- Close down our Early Years Factory that moves so many from destined-for-success to life-of-struggles.
- End our ongoing flood of struggling readers and Spelling Generations.
- Attain the easier, highly effective education that many other nations routinely achieve.

Our latest census showed commonest Aussies are parents who have finished Year 12 at school, and have two children.

Let's invest in those children, in every Aussie who finishes high school, and in every parent of the future, by improving education exponentially, using 10 Changes improvements, so we then meet our teaching challenges extremely well.

Keep Change Thinking Happening

You never change things by fighting the existing reality. To change something, build a new model that makes the existing model obsolete.

R Buckminster Fuller[xlix]

The secret of getting ahead is getting started.

Mark Twain[l]

Thank you so much for joining me in this discussion.

Our current education struggles are a complex, multifaceted problem with many underlying factors. In having been so intractable and difficult to resolve, despite the massive efforts we've expended, they're a major challenge.

Many great minds have reflected and debated our struggles at length. Many suggested solutions have been trialled. But our problems continue.

As Winston Churchill[li] once said, with regard to Russia, it's *a riddle wrapped in a mystery inside an enigma; but perhaps there is a key.*

Echoing Churchill, perhaps there is a key. We must reflect on the many and varied impacts of English orthographic complexity, an insufficiently considered, key factor that is pivotally important in perpetuating our reading, literacy and education struggles, and rendering current, would-be effective solutions far less so.

Please keep change-thinking happening.

Australia needs you.

Please keep the discussion on 10 Changes issues going with family, friends and colleagues. And once it's begun, please keep our needed improvement-actioning happening as well.

The future is bright. Let's move there.

The strength of any new theory lies in the accuracy of its predictions, its beauty in its simplicity, and its importance in the depth and breadth of its application.

Dale Bredesen[lii]

Acknowledgements

My heartfelt thanks to all who have helped so much in my learning and authoring journey.

To the children and families I've worked with, thank you!

Thank you too, to the many teachers, researchers and academics with whom I've worked and had discussions.

To Prof Bruce Knight, Central Queensland University (CQU), and all staff I've worked with – I thank you.

To all who have encouraged me in writing the *Aussie Reading Woes* trilogy, many thanks.

To my friends and colleagues who read my extremely long, earliest draft, which was the basis for *Bunyips* and its *Aussie Reading Woes* partners, and gave me such valuable feedback, thank you – your efforts are hugely appreciated.

And my most heartfelt and special thanks to Bev, Mark and Marion, Laura and Glenys, who have done the long haul with me, for your many, many, many hours of reading, critiquing, editing and support.

And to my precious family – thank you so much for all and everything.

Also by Susan Galletly

1. **BOOK: *The Research Tours: The Impacts of Orthographic Disadvantage*.**
   Book 2 of the *Aussie Reading Woes* series.
   Galletly, S. A., 2023. Literacy Plus, Australia.
2. **BOOK: *The 10 Changes: The Nitty Gritty*.**
   Book 3 of the *Aussie Reading Woes* series.
   Galletly, S. A., 2023. Literacy Plus, Australia.
3. **The Literacy Component Model: A pragmatic universal paradigm**.
   Knight, B. A., Galletly, S. A., & Aprile, K. T., 2021. *International Journal of Innovation, Creativity and Change, 15*(7).
4. **Bridging the gap between reading theory and teacher practice**.
   Knight, B. A., Galletly, S. A., & Gargett, P. S., 2020. *International Journal of Innovation, Creativity, & Change, 13*(8), 1-19.
5. **Practical school-level implications of cognitive processing and cognitive load**. Knight, B. A., & Galletly, S. A., 2020. In A. M. Columbus (Ed.), *Advances in psychology research* (Vol. 140, pp. 1-90). Nova Science Publishers.
6. **The shifting landscape of text and how it is comprehended**.
   Knight, B. A., & Galletly, S. A., 2020. In P. Bagoly-Simo & Z. Sikorova. (Eds.), *Textbooks and educational media: Perspectives from subject education* (pp. 47-58). Springer.

7. **Orthographic Advantage Theory: National advantage and disadvantage due to orthographic differences.**
   Knight, B. A., Galletly, S. A., & Gargett, P. S., 2019. *Asia Pacific Journal of Developmental Differences, 6*(1, Jan), 5-29.

8. **Reading instruction strategies to reduce cognitive load.**
   Knight, B. A., Galletly, S. A., Morris, J., & Gargett, P. S., 2018. *Practical Literacy: The Early and Primary Years, 23*(2), 8-10.

9. **Effective literacy instruction for all students: A time for change.**
   Knight, B. A., & Galletly, S. A., 2017. *International J. for Research in Learning Disabilities 3*(1), 65-86.

10. **Managing cognitive load as the key to literacy development: Research directions suggested by crosslinguistic research and research on Initial Teaching Alphabet (i.t.a.).**
    Knight, B. A., Galletly, S. A., & Gargett, P. S., 2017. In R. Nata (Ed.), *Progress in education* (Vol. 45, pp. 61-150). Nova Science Publishers.

11. **Principles of reading instruction towards optimising reading instruction for at-risk readers in Prep to Year 3: Principles developed through teacher reflection on research and practice in the ARC project 'Bridging the Gap for At-Risk Readers: Reading Theory into Classroom Practice'.**
    Knight, B. A., Galletly, S. A., & Gargett, P. S., 2017. Central Queensland University.

12. **The effects of an intervention program on middle school students' literacy skills.**
    Knight, B. A., & Galletly, S. A., 2016. *Special Education Perspectives, 25*(1), 7-17.

13. **Because trucks aren't bicycles: Orthographic complexity as a disregarded variable in reading research.** Galletly, S. A., & Knight, B. A., 2013. *Australian Educational Researcher, 40*(2), 173-194.

14. **Differential disadvantage of Anglophone weak readers with language and cognitive processing weakness.**
    Galletly, S. A., & Knight, B. A., 2011. *Australasian Journal of Special Education, 35*(1), 72-96.

15. **Transition from early to sophisticated literacy as a factor in cross-national achievement differences.**
    Galletly, S. A., & Knight, B. A., 2011. *Australian Educational Researcher, 38*, 329-354.

16. **Developing an informed and integrated teaching approach for students with reading-accuracy difficulties in the primary school.**
    Knight, B. A., & Galletly, S. A., 2011. In D. Lynch & B. A. Knight (Eds.), *Issues in contemporary teaching* (Vol. 2, pp. 65-89). AACLM Press.

17. *CQUniversity Accelerated Metacognitive Literacy Intensive Tuition (CAMLIT): Program for middle school students experiencing literacy difficulties.*
    Galletly, S. A., & Knight, B. A., 2010. Central Queensland University.

18. **When tests frame children: The challenges of providing appropriate education for children with special needs.**
    Galletly, S. A., Knight, B. A., & Dekkers, J., 2010. *Australasian J. of Special Education, 34*(2), 133-154.

19. **Indicators of late emerging reading-accuracy difficulties in Australian schools.**
    Galletly, S. A., Knight, B. A., Dekkers, J., & Galletly, T. A., 2009. *The Australian Journal of Teacher Education, 34*(5), 54-64.

20. *An exploration of rapid-use reading-accuracy tests in an Australian context (Doctoral Thesis)*
    Galletly, S. A., 2008.
    Central Queensland University.

21. **The *Dynamic Indicators of Early Literacy Skills* (DIBELS) used in an Australian context.**
    Galletly, S. A., & Knight, B. A., 2006. *Australian Journal of Learning Disabilities, 11*(3), 147-154.

22. **The *Test of Word Reading Efficiency (TOWRE)* used in an Australian context.**
    Knight, B. A., & Galletly, S. A., 2006. *Australian Journal of Learning Disabilities, 11*(3), 139-146.

23. **The role of metacognition in reading-accuracy learning and instruction.**
    Knight, B. A., & Galletly, S. A., 2005. *Australian Journal of Learning Disabilities, 10*(2), 63-70.

24. **The high cost of orthographic disadvantage.**
    Galletly, S. A., & Knight, B. A., 2004. *Australian Journal of Learning Disabilities, 9*(4), 4-11.

25. **The Galletly Report: Reading-accuracy development, difficulties and instruction in Australia: Report submitted to the Australian National Inquiry into the Teaching of Literacy.**
    Galletly, S. A., 2005. Central Queensland University.

26. **Reading accuracy and phonological recoding: Poor relations no longer.**
    Galletly, S. A., 2004. In B. Knight & W. Scott (Eds.), *Learning disabilities: Multiple perspectives*. Pearson Education Australia.

27. **The challenge: Improving core literacy outcomes in Education Queensland schools.**
    Galletly, S. A., 2002. In B. Knight (Ed.), *Reconceptualising knowledge in the knowledge society* (pp. 1-16). Post Pressed.

28. **Making a real difference: Supporting children with learning disabilities.**
    Galletly, S. A., 2001. *Australian Communication Quarterly, 3*(1).

29. **BOOK: *Two Vowels Talking: Keys to literacy progress*.**
    Galletly, S. A., 2001. Literacy Plus, Australia.

30. **CD/DVD: The Literacy Plus CD (Professional development videos).**
    Galletly, S. A., 2000. Literacy Plus, Australia.

31. **BOOK: *Phonological Fun*.**
    Galletly, S. A., 2000. Literacy Plus, Australia.

32. **Phonological fun: The prereading challenge.**
    Galletly, S. A., 2000. In D. Greaves & D. Barwood (Eds.), *Creating positive futures: Strategies & methods for those who learn differently.* Australian Resource Educators' Association.

33. **BOOK: *Sounds & Vowels: Keys to literacy progress.***
    Galletly, S. A., 1999. Literacy Plus, Australia.

34. **Analogies for explaining information processing.**
    Galletly, S. A., 1999. In S. McLeod & L. McAllister (Eds.), *Towards 2000: Embracing change, challenge and choice: Proceedings of the 1999 Speech Pathology Australia National Conference.* Speech Pathology Australia.

35. **Making a lasting difference: The 'phonological + literacy' combination.**
    Galletly, S. A., 1999. In P. Westwood & W. Scott (Eds.), *Learning disabilities advocacy and action: Proceedings of the 1999 National Conference of the Australian Resource Educators Association.* AREA.

For more on Susan's writing, visit
www.literacyplus.com.au

Quote Sources

[i] Jackie French (2015) Acceptance speech for the 2015 Older Australian of the Year Award, www.youtube.com/watch?v=Kuc4GUfE3lM.

[ii] Aristotle, https://www.goodreads.com/author/quotes/2192.Aristotle.

[iii] Kher, U. (2001, March 26). Deconstructing dyslexia: Blame it on the written word. *Time Magazine*, p.56.

[iv] Nelson Mandela, https://thefourthrevolution.org/wordpress/archives/4281.

[v] Jackie French (2015), as cited above.

[vi] Robert F Kennedy, who often paraphrased George Bernard Shaw's words (in *Back to Methuselah*), e.g., in *Remarks at the University of Kansas*, March 18, 1968.

[vii] Thomas Edison, https://everydaypowerblog.com/thomas-edison-quotes/.

[viii] Harold Koplewicz, H. (2010). Orlando Bloom on dyslexia (Adam Katz Memorial Lecture). *Child Mind Institute*. childmind.org/article/orlando-bloom-on-dyslexia/.

[ix] Brendan Nelson, Federal Minister for Education, 2005. Launch of the reports of Australia's *National Inquiry into the Teaching of Literacy* Department of Education Science and Training, www.dest.gov.au.

[x] Mikko Aro (2004). *Learning to read: The effect of orthography*. University of Jyvaskyla, Finland.

[xi] Richard Venezky (2004). In search of the perfect orthography. *Written Language & Literacy*, 7(2), 39-63.

[xii] Mikko Aro (2004), as cited above.

[xiii] Esther Geva and Linda Siegel (2000). Orthographic and cognitive factors in the concurrent development of basic reading skills in two languages. *Reading and Writing: An Interdisciplinary Journal, 12*(1), 1-30.

[xivxiv] Jackie French (2015), as cited above.

[xv] John Dewey (1916). Democracy and Education, https://www.gutenberg.org/files/852/852-h/852-h.htm.

[xvi] Bruce Knight, Susan Galletly & Pamela Gargett (2019). Orthographic Advantage Theory: National advantage and disadvantage due to orthographic differences. *Asia Pacific Journal of Developmental Differences, 6*(1, January), 5-29.

[xvii] Geoff Masters (2016). Five challenges in Australian school education. *Policy Insights, May*, 1-32. http://research.acer.edu.au.

[xviii] Geoff Masters (2016), as cited above.

[xix] Jackie French (2015), as cited above.

[xx] Richard Venezky (2004), as cited above.

[xxi] Nelson Mandela, https://thefourthrevolution.org/wordpress/archives/4281.

[xxii] National People with Disabilities and Carer Council. (2009). *Shut out: The experience of people with disabilities and their families in Australia: National Disability Strategy Consultation Report.* www.dss.gov.au.

[xxiii] Bruce Knight and Susan Galletly (2017). Effective literacy instruction for all students: A time for change. *International Journal for Research in Learning Disabilities* 3(1), 65-86.

[xxiv] Australian Education Act 2013. Australian Government, www.legislation.gov.au. Quoted and discussed in Knight & Galletly (2017), cited above.

[xxv] Senate Standing Committee on Education and Employment. (2016). *Access to real learning: The impact of policy, funding and culture on students with disability.* www.aph.gov.au. Quoted and discussed in Knight & Galletly (2017), above.

[xxvi] Bill Walsh, in Walsh, Jamison & Walsh (2009). *The score takes care of itself: My philosophy of leadership,* Penguin Books.

[xxvii] Carol McDonald Connor et al., (2004). Beyond the Reading Wars: Exploring the effect of child-instruction interactions on growth in early reading. *Scientific Studies of Reading,* 8(4), 305-336.

[xxviii] Steven Maier & Martin Seligman (2016). Learned Helplessness at fifty: Insights from neuroscience. *Psychological Review,* 123(4), 349-367.

[xxix] Susan Galletly and Bruce Knight (2011). Differential disadvantage of Anglophone weak readers with language and cognitive processing weakness. *Australasian Journal of Special Education,* 35(1), 72-96.

[xxx] Richard Branson in online interview: Source no longer available online, but quite likely an interview with 12 year old Australian girl, Isley, who had earlier posted online a great video, *Like a Dyslexic:* https://www.dyslexiadaily.com/blog/like-a-dyslexic-12-year-old-isley-video-worth-sharing/.

[xxxi] Plutarch, a contraction of his original words in *Moralia, On listening to lectures* https://conversational-leadership.net/quotation/mind-vessel-fire-kindled/.

[xxxii] Carl Jung (1942). *The gifted child,* in his book, The development of personality (1954).

[xxxiii] Daniel Quinn (1999) *Beyond civilization : Humanity's next great adventure.* Three Rivers Press, New York.

[xxxiv] R. Buckminster Fuller (1965) *World Design Science Decade: Phase 1 Document 3: Comprehensive Thinking.* World Resources Inventory: World Design Science Decade 1965-1975. Southern Illinois University.

[xxxv] Frank Warburton and Vera Southgate (1969). *I.T.A.: An independent evaluation.* Newgate Publishers, London.

[xxxvi] Thomas Edison, https://everydaypowerblog.com/thomas-edison-quotes/.

[xxxvii] H.S. Huang and J Richard Hanley (1997). A longitudinal study of phonological awareness, visual skills, and Chinese reading acquisition among first-graders in Taiwan. *International Journal of Behavioural Development*, 20(2), 249-268.

[xxxviii] Frank Warburton & Vera Southgate (1969), as cited above.

[xxxix] Professor Sir Cyril Burt (1969). Foreword to Warburton & Southgate (1969) 'i.t.a.: An independent evaluation' (pp. pp. iv-vii).

[xl] Albert J Mazurkiewicz (1973). *i.t.a. Revisited* Annual Meeting of the College Reading Assn. (17th, Silver Springs), www.eric.gov.

[xli] Albert J Mazurkiewicz (1965). The initial teaching alphabet for reading? Yes! *Educational Leadership*, *22*(6), 390-438, www.eric.gov.

[xlii] George Santayana, https://playart.org/philosophy.php.

[xliii] Leo F. Buscaglia, https://bukrate.com/author/leo-f-buscaglia-quotes?p=3.

[xliv] Geoff Masters (2016), as cited above.

[xlv] Jackie French (2015), as cited above.

[xlvi][xlvi] Thomas Edison, https://everydaypowerblog.com/thomas-edison-quotes/.

[xlvii] Thomas Edison, https://everydaypowerblog.com/thomas-edison-quotes/.

[xlviii] Nelson Mandela, https://socialimpactarchitects.com/nelson-mandela-dreams/.

[xlix] R Buckminster Fuller, source uncertain, possibly in Fuller, Agel & Fiore (1970) *I seem to be a verb*. Bantam Books.

[l] Mark Twain, https://upjourney.com/mark-twain-quotes.

[li] Winston Churchill (1939, 1 October), BBC radio broadcast.

[lii] Dale Bredesen (2017). *The end of Alzheimer's*. Avery Publishers, New York.

www.ingramcontent.com/pod-product-compliance
Lightning Source LLC
Chambersburg PA
CBHW051940290426
44110CB00015B/2052